P9-DFJ-685

365
Read to Me
Prayers
for Children

By Melanie M. Burnette

BROADMAN
&HOLMAN
PUBLISHERS

Nashville, Tennessee

© 1999 Ottenheimer Publishers, Inc.
All rights reserved
Published by Broadman & Holman Publishers
127 Ninth Avenue, North, Nashville TN 37234
under arrangement with Ottenheimer Publishers, Inc.
Printed in the United States of America
BI122M L K J I H G F E D C B A

This book is dedicated in loving memory of my father, William A. "Bill" Mason

Note to Parents

Is there anything more innocent, more wondrous, than a child's prayer to God? Children are so honest and enthusiastic when they pray. Their wishes for their loved ones, friends, and even pets are so heartfelt. They believe that if they ask God to bless their grandmother or their fish or even their favorite baseball glove, God is listening to every word. And the most wonderful thing is—that's true!

But prayer can be even more than a wish list. It can be a good time to reflect on feelings, dilemmas, and things that happen in everyday life. This book, *365 Read-to-Me Prayers for Children*, opens young readers up to new ways to pray. Through references to the best-loved stories of the Bible, it shows children how what happens to them at home, at school, with family members and friends, isn't so very different from what Biblical people went through in their own struggles and relationships. By showing how these ancient people dealt with life's ups and downs, the book gives children ideas for their own conversations with God and new ways of thinking about their own situations.

Is your child dealing with feelings of jealousy and anger toward a sibling? Here children will read about Cain and Abel, and how the narrator asks God for help in getting over similar feelings, if they ever happen. Is your child experiencing grief over the death of a loved one or pet? Through prayers that mention the deaths of Sarah, Isaac, Moses, Jesus, and other characters, children will see how God will be with them through everything, helping them work through the sadness. Whether your child is feeling joy for a job well done or a kind word from a teacher, or insecurity about what is right and wrong, he or she will find something to relate to in *365 Read-to-Me Prayers*.

You can help your children benefit the most from this book by reading one prayer every day of the year. You may want to incorporate these readings into their nightly prayers. A companion book, *365 Read-to-Me Bedtime Bible Stories*, includes the stories featured in this book and can be very helpful to understanding these prayers. However, the prayers provide enough background on the best-loved Bible stories that this book can stand alone, if necessary.

Most importantly, if your children do not understand something, be open to answer questions the best way you can. You know your children better than anyone, so you are the best person to apply the prayers to their daily lives. Have a Bible handy so you can refer to the stories as needed. Listen to and enjoy your children's prayers. This is the time when they are building a foundation of communicating with God that will last a lifetime.

One of the most incredible gifts we receive from God is His willingness to listen to us and hear our hopes, dreams, concerns, and wishes through prayer. How wonderful it is that, despite the vastness of the earth and all its people, every grownup and every child can talk to God directly any time. Truly, God's desire that we seek His wisdom and guidance through prayer is evidence of His great love for us.

Prayer 1

Genesis 1–2

Without You, God, there would be no world. Your goodness is all around us. Each day, let the song of the birds and the whisper of the wind remind me of Your greatness and the love You show in giving us such a beautiful home. Dear Lord, thank You for this wonderful earth You created.

Prayer 2

Genesis 1–2

Lord, help me to take care of this world as You wanted Adam to. Help me to understand that because You took earth and made Adam from it, I am a part of creation and I have been given the job of looking after the earth. And God, help me to care for all the creatures of the world and to protect the land that You have given us.

Prayer 3

Genesis 3

Dear God, help me to turn away from evil. I know it can wear many disguises, so it can tempt me to lie or be mean to others. In the Garden of Eden You told Adam and Eve not to eat the fruit of the tree of knowledge of good and evil. But Satan, taking the form of a snake, told Eve she would become wise if she took a bite of fruit from the tree. Eve wanted to be wise, so she made a great mistake and ate the fruit. She did not put her faith and trust in You and did not follow Your rules. Please stay close to me, Lord, and guide me away from Satan's path.

Prayer 4

Genesis 3

Lord, please forgive us our sins. And help us not to blame others when things go wrong. When You asked Adam and Eve if they had eaten the forbidden fruit, Adam blamed Eve. You told Adam and Eve that they had to leave the Garden of Eden and go out in the world. You said they would have to work very hard to stay alive. Dear Lord, help me to see that when I make mistakes—and we all do—I should take responsibility for them.

Prayer 5

Genesis 4

Heavenly Father, help me to have a kind heart. Adam and Eve's sons Cain and Abel taught us a valuable lesson about right and wrong ways to behave. Cain was angry and jealous of his brother, but Abel was loving. When they made sacrifices to You, God, Abel's sacrifice pleased You, and You praised him for it. Cain got very angry because he thought his sacrifice was just as good. Cain could not be happy for his brother's success. Lord, please help me to be happy for others when good things happen to them.

Prayer 6

Genesis 4

Lord, it's terrible when brothers and sisters don't get along. Cain got so angry when he thought You loved Abel best that he killed his own brother. I pray today that brothers and sisters all over the world will learn to love one another and settle their arguments peaceably. It's important to get along!

Prayer 7

Genesis 6

After Cain was sent away for killing Abel, evil began to spread across the land. Noah was one of the good people. He kept on believing in You, God. Because of Noah's good example, we know that if we are willing to do what You ask of us—no matter how hard it seems at first—good things will come to us in the end. Let the ark be a sign of hope for us all. Thank You, Lord, for Noah's strong faith.

Prayer 8

Genesis 7

Lord, people may sometimes make fun of me for believing in You. I know that You are always with me, though. When Noah was building his ark just as You told him to, people came by and laughed at him. He tried to warn them to stop their bad ways and follow You, but they would not listen. Dear God, help me to keep my faith even when others don't understand.

Prayer 9

Genesis 8

It's not easy to wait for something that we want very badly. Noah and his family must have gotten very tired of living on that boat for so long. But they waited for Your sign that it was safe to leave the ark, and You kept them safe. Sometimes I have trouble waiting. I feel like I can't wait to be older so I can have my own room or walk to school by myself. Please teach me to be patient, dear God.

Prayer 10

Genesis 9

Dear God, here is a poem for You:

The rainbow high above us,
So colorful and free.
When we look upon it,
It's Your love we see.

You gave Your word to Noah
That never would there be
A flood to destroy all things on earth.
That's good enough for me.

Dear Lord, please help me to appreciate the world every day, which You made better after the flood.

Prayer 11

Genesis 11

Heavenly Father, help us to understand one another. When Noah's grown sons and daughters tried to build a tower just for their own kind, You were unhappy. You mixed up all the languages so the people could not understand each other.

When we meet someone who we think is unlike us or who doesn't speak our language, dear Lord, help us to remember to be kind even to those who are different from us.

Prayer 12

Genesis 11–12

Dear Lord, I pray for the strength to follow Your plan for me even if it's not always the easiest or most popular way. When You asked Abraham and Sarah to leave their home in the city and take their nephew, Lot, to Canaan, it must have been hard for them to leave their comfortable life behind. But they had faith in You and trusted You. God, please help me to understand that Your love is more important than all the things I have.

Prayer 13

Genesis 13

Many times I want to keep the best things for myself, but I know it is better to be unselfish. Abraham was very generous to let Lot choose first when they were dividing the land You had given them. May I, too, learn to experience the joys of giving and sharing. Lord, when I make choices, please help me to think of others and what they might want, too.

Prayer 14

Genesis 14–15

Abraham and Sarah wanted so much to have children, but they thought they were too old. Still, You had promised them a child. Dear Lord, help us to have faith even when something seems impossible. You want us to pray to You and to trust You. If we do that, You have promised to care for us always. Our Heavenly Father, You are so wonderful to keep the promises You have made to Your people. I pray that I always remember to turn to You first.

Prayer 15

Genesis 16

Sometimes it's hard to be patient while I wait for Your promises to come true, dear Lord. It's easy to give up hope. After Abraham and Sarah waited so long to have a child, they began to doubt Your promise. They even came up with a plan so Abraham could have a child with Sarah's servant, Hagar. Hagar had a child, Ishmael, but this was not Your plan. Let me wait patiently for Your plans, dear God. Show me each day the things You want me to do.

Prayer 16

Genesis 17–18

Dear Lord, help me to always be open to You. At times when something may seem strange or even unbelievable it is really You trying to send me a message. Sarah laughed when a visitor told her she would have a son. Then she found out the visitor was You! You were right, too—she had a son named Isaac. I pray to always know in my heart that with You to help me, nothing is impossible. I know that whether I'm taking a test or running a race, I can ask for Your help, trust You with my problems, and know You're always there. Thank You, Heavenly Father, for being there for me.

Prayer 17

Genesis 18–19

Dear Lord, we want to obey our parents and teachers, but we don't always do this. It is so easy to do whatever seems fun at the time. Sometimes we don't understand that we could be badly hurt if we do something we're not supposed to do. The same thing happens when we don't obey You, dear Father. When Lot and his wife were told to leave their city because it was going to be destroyed, they almost waited too long. Lot's wife even turned to look back when the angels told her not to. She was turned into a pillar of salt. You always know what is best for us. Help us to obey You, our parents, and our teachers, every day.

Prayer 18

Genesis 19

When bad things happen, I get very sad, dear God. I wonder why things have to be the way they are. I forget that everything is part of Your plan. Lot must have been very sad about losing his wife and home, but he was also grateful that You had let him get the rest of his family out in time. Lord, when I'm sad, remind me that good things are just around the corner. Please take away my sadness and fill me with Your love.

Prayer 19

Genesis 21

Dear God, my brothers and sisters and I don't always get along. When we're angry, we forget how much we love each other. Isaac and Ishmael must have had a hard time sharing their parents' love. Even Sarah was jealous of Ishmael. But You said that

You would take care of both of Abraham's sons and that You love all children equally. Please bless my brothers and sisters. Help me to show my love for them every day.

Prayer 20

Genesis 21

Dear Lord, Abraham's son Isaac came to lead the people now considered the Jews. His son Ishmael came to lead the people now known as the Arabs. If they had been allowed to grow up as brothers instead of as enemies, maybe there wouldn't be so much war today. Instead, because they were stepbrothers and their mothers were jealous of each other, Isaac and Ishmael were forced apart. Some days, I see bad things on the news or hear about fighting in other countries. I pray for the people in these countries, dear God. I pray especially for the children who are too young to understand what war is all about. Please help them to grow up in peace.

Prayer 21

Genesis 22

When You test my faith, dear God, please help me to be strong. Abraham must have been very afraid when You asked him to sacrifice his own son Isaac. But his faith was so strong, he was ready to obey You. Of course, You were not really going to make Abraham kill his son—You were only testing his faith. You were happy then that Abraham showed You he was truly a man of God. It's hard for people to trust in things they can't see, but I know You are with me. Keep me strong every day, dear Father.

Prayer 22

Genesis 24

People have traveled many miles to do Your will, dear God. The trips must have seemed long and lonely, especially back in Bible times when people lived so far from each other. Please help me to understand that sometimes I must go that extra mile to do what is right, just as when Isaac's servant traveled so far to find Isaac a bride who loved You, God. The right way is not always the easy way! I pray that I always know that with Your help, I can do anything.

Prayer 23

Genesis 24

Dear God, Isaac's servant knew he would find the right woman for Isaac. She would be the one who offered his camels water. Sure enough, Rebekah did this very thing! You had sent him a sign. As I grow up, I will meet many new people, dear Lord. Please lead me to the ones who will help me to learn more about You. And God, please help me to know when You are sending me a sign.

Prayer 24

Genesis 24

What a joyful day it is when Your will is done, dear Lord! You sent Rebekah to Isaac to be his wife. They were both blessed because they trusted in You. Thank You, Lord, for Your many blessings.

Prayer 25

Genesis 25

When we give to others, Heavenly Father, help us to do so unselfishly. Let us give from our hearts and not ask for anything in return. Isaac and Rebekah must have been very surprised to have twins. Unfortunately, only one son could inherit most of the father's wealth in those days. Jacob was not acting very brotherly when he tried to trick his twin, Esau, into trading his inheritance for a bowl of stew. I pray that You show us how to be loving and generous, dear Lord.

Prayer 26

Genesis 27

Lord, sometimes my friends and I play foolish tricks on each other. We put on masks and try to scare each other, or we say we did something when we really didn't. But Rebekah went beyond a practical joke. Jacob was her favorite son, so she wanted him to inherit Isaac's money. She had Jacob wear goat skins on his hands and pretend to be Esau, whose skin was hairy. Isaac, who was almost blind, then gave his blessing to the wrong twin. Rebekah and Jacob were wrong to trick Isaac, who was a fair man. Dear God, please help me to be honest with my family and friends. I know that in Your eyes, it is always better to tell the truth than to trick someone. Also, help me realize I won't always get what I want.

Prayer 27

Genesis 27

Our Father, when Jacob tricked Isaac, Isaac was sad. He wanted Jacob to find a woman of God, who would help him learn to do what was right. I know what he meant—some of my friends do the right thing, and some always seem to be in trouble. When I'm with those who obey, it's easier for me to be good. Please lead me to people who will help me do the right thing; but when I am with others who want me to do the wrong thing, help me to tell them no, dear Lord.

Prayer 28

Genesis 28

How thankful we are that You are always willing to forgive us, O Lord. Even Jacob, who had tricked his brother and made him unhappy, was blessed with Your forgiveness. No matter what time of day or night, You speak to us and fill us with Your love. I pray that You will guide me toward redemption as You guided Jacob.

Prayer 29

Genesis 29

Please help me to be patient, dear Lord. Sometimes I want something and I feel I must get it *now*. Jacob was willing to wait fourteen years for Rachel, whom he loved! I hope that I learn to wait for things and to trust You to answer my prayers, Lord, even though it might not happen right away.

Prayer 30

Genesis 30–31

Please keep me from harm, dear Lord. Keep me away from people who would hurt me or cheat me. When Jacob had to run away from his father-in-law who had tricked him many times, he must have been afraid. But You had promised him that he would live to have many children and rule over great lands. Jacob had faith in You. Show me Your way, dear God, and keep me safe as I follow it.

Prayer 31

Genesis 32

Dear Lord, when Jacob was on his way home, he got in a wrestling match with a man. He didn't know it was You, Lord. I pray that I am able to live my life as if You are always watching. Let me pay attention to what I do and say, because You are always right beside me. Sometimes I might be surprised at what disguises You take. I won't be frightened as long as You are with me, Lord.

Prayer 32

Genesis 33

Thank You for my family, Lord. We are important to each other, even though we may not always get along. Help me to know that even when I fight with someone in my family, we can make up, no matter how hard it seems. In the Bible, Jacob and Esau treated each other badly when they were young; but later, with Your help, they forgave each other. Please bless families all over the world, dear God, and help me to appreciate my family.

Prayer 33

Genesis 35

Dear Lord, please help those who have lost a loved one. It's very sad when someone dies. Jacob must have really missed Rachel when she went to heaven. They had been married such a long time. When people lose someone they love, please comfort them in their sadness, dear Lord. Show them that they are never really alone because You are with them.

Prayer 34

Genesis 37

Dear Lord, if I have a toy or a pair of sneakers that is better than someone else's, I shouldn't brag about it. That makes other people jealous. Even though Joseph didn't think he was showing off when he got his beautiful coat of many colors, his brothers felt left out. Help me not to be boastful, O Lord. I pray that I will respect the feelings of others when I talk about my life.

Prayer 35

Genesis 37

You have taught us that jealousy can be a very bad thing, dear Lord. It makes brothers hate each other and do mean things to each other. Help me not to feel jealous if my brother or friend seems to have things I don't have. Joseph's brothers were selfish. They could not be happy for him. I pray that I will be able to enjoy the good things that happen to others.

Prayer 36

Genesis 37

Dear Lord, if I am with others who want to do something wrong, please help me to be like Reuben. He knew it was wrong to hurt his brother Joseph. He kept his brothers from killing Joseph, but he couldn't stop them from sending Joseph away. The other boys told their father that Joseph was dead, which made him very sad. Lying and hurting others ends up making everyone unhappy. Please help me to be truthful, dear Lord.

Prayer 37

Genesis 39

I'm so glad that You always believe in me, God—even if other people don't. When I am telling the truth You know it because You know all and see all. Joseph must have felt good to know that even in bad times

You would never leave him. Our world doesn't always make sense. At least I know You are there to help me to get through whatever may happen. Thank You for Your loyalty, dear God.

Prayer 38

Genesis 40

You have given us all special talents, dear Lord. Some of us are good spellers. Others do well in music or science. Some people can sing beautifully. Joseph's talent was that he could tell people what their dreams meant. I pray that I will take the special talent You have given me and use it to help others in some way, Heavenly Father.

Prayer 39

Genesis 41

It is important to remember that our talents come from You, dear God. Some kids think that because they can run fast or make straight As, they are better than the rest of us. When Pharaoh asked Joseph if he could tell people what their dreams meant, Joseph answered, "I can't do it myself, but God will help me." I pray that I can be humble, too, and give You credit when it is Yours.

Prayer 40

Genesis 41

Dear God, today is an important day to be lived and enjoyed, but help me learn that I must plan for tomorrow too. Let me do good things each day to make others happy. Then, at the end of the day, let me make a little plan for tomorrow. That way I can help make sure that tomorrow will go well too. Joseph was smart to warn Pharaoh that he must prepare for a famine after a time of good crops. Bless my plans, Heavenly Father, so that they will be pleasing to You.

Prayer 41

Genesis 42

Sharing with my friends makes me feel good about myself, dear Lord. I like the look on my friend's face when I hand her the toy I've been playing with. She smiles the same way I smile at her when she shares some cookies with me. Sharing has to go both ways. Joseph's brothers expected him to share his grain with them, but they had been mean to him when he was younger and hadn't shared with him. Joseph wanted to teach his brothers a little lesson when they came to see him and didn't know who he was, so he put them in prison. Every day I pray You will open up my heart so I'll be willing to share, dear Lord.

Prayer 42

Genesis 42

Some people think they can hurt others and get away with it. You know what is in every person's heart, dear God. Nobody who harms others really gets away with it because You will judge everyone's actions. Joseph's brother Reuben knew that. Even though Reuben did not recognize Joseph at first, he believed that when the governor of Egypt put him and his brothers in prison, they were being punished for wronging Joseph in the past. All those years he must have felt bad about what they had done. Please help me to know right from wrong so I never disappoint You.

Prayer 43

Genesis 43

Missing someone we care for is hard,
dear Lord. Thank You for bringing so many
people back together again. Joseph was so
happy to see his youngest brother, Benjamin,
that he had to leave the room so he could
hide his feelings. What a joy it is when we
see a friend or loved one again! You are so
kind to bring brothers back together again,
but when that's not possible, we know Your
grace will provide comfort. Please help
those whose loved ones have been away
from home for a long time.

Prayer 44

Genesis 44

Most of us have plenty to eat, dear Lord,
even if it's not always the things we like.
Joseph was generous to give his grain to his
brothers. He knew how terrible it is to go

to sleep with no dinner. When we're eating our meals, let us stop and be thankful for what we have. I pray tonight for anyone who is hungry.

Prayer 45

Genesis 44–45

It is such a blessing to forgive others, dear Lord! When people do mean things to others, most people try to think of ways to hurt them. Joseph was very nice to tell his brothers not to feel guilty. He knew that You had sent him, Lord, to take care of them during the time of no food. Sometimes we can't help being mad, and it's hard to forgive someone who's been mean. But with Your help, Lord, we can learn to forgive others as You forgive us. Thank You, dear God, for Your generous heart.

Prayer 46

Genesis 45–50

Dear God, many dads are loving and caring. Some love their children but don't always let them know it. Other dads care, but they can't be around to spend time with their children—just like Jacob couldn't be with Joseph for much of his life. Even when we can't be with our own fathers, we know we have You, our Heavenly Father, to take care of us all. Bless my dad, dear Lord, and bless all the other fathers in the world.

Prayer 47

Exodus 1

Dear Lord, please help me to treat all people equally. Some people come from faraway lands. They may look different or sound strange when they speak, but inside, we are all alike. The new Pharaoh didn't like the Israelites just because they were foreigners. I pray that I will be understanding when someone isn't just like me.

Prayer 48

Exodus 2

Dear God, thank You for saving baby Moses! After his mother had sent him down the stream in a basket to protect him from Pharaoh, she was very happy when she knew baby Moses was safe. Please help mothers and babies everywhere, dear Lord. Keep them safe from harm.

Prayer 49

Exodus 2

Dear Lord, help me to do a good deed for someone today. As a young man, Moses helped people many times. He was brave in the face of bullies. If I have to face a bully at school or walk by those children who say ugly things about me behind my back, I know You are with me, dear Lord. I will trust You to protect me and to show me how to live peaceably with those I don't get along with.

Prayer 50

Exodus 3

Dear Lord, You are so amazing that You can even command things in creation. When You wanted to show Moses a sign, You made a bush burn and a stick turn into a snake. These signs let Moses know that You truly are the God of us all. Then You gave these powers to Moses, so he could spread the word of God to others. Please help me to understand Your great power, dear Father.

Prayer 51

Exodus 4–5

Dear Lord, sometimes, when I'm trying to learn something new or to help my mom and dad, I mess it up, even though I mean well. Help me to see that if I keep trying, I will get the hang of it, especially with Your help. Moses was upset when the Pharaoh wouldn't let the Israelites go and even gave them more work. He thought he had made things worse for them, but You told him it would work out. You will always do what is best for us, dear Lord. Please help me to have patience when something I want to do doesn't work out the first time.

Prayer 52

Exodus 7–9

Some people in this world think they have all the power, dear Lord. Leaders of armies and governments have so much money and so many followers that they begin to think they are the rulers of the earth. Pharaoh refused to believe in You even after many plagues and disasters happened to his people. I am grateful that You are the only real leader, Lord, and I respect Your power.

Prayer 53

Exodus 10–11

Dear God, I'm being stubborn when I have an idea about how something should be and I stick with it even if I'm wrong. Sometimes I want to have my way no matter what. Pharaoh was very stubborn when he would not let the Israelites go, as Moses asked. Every time Moses and Aaron sent a sign from You, Pharaoh's heart grew harder and harder. Help me not to be stubborn, dear Lord, because I know Your way is always the best.

Prayer 54

Exodus 12

As some of us celebrate Passover, we thank You for all the promises You've kept, dear Lord. Your mercy saved the children of the Israelites. Thank You for guiding us and protecting us every day. We thank You for Your blessings, dear God.

Prayer 55

Exodus 12

Dear Lord, it must have been scary for the Israelites to watch all the terrible things that were happening around them in Egypt. Sometimes the story of the Israelites reminds me of what's happening in our world with pollution, hunger, and violence. But the Israelites' faith in You was strong and You helped them, just as You said You would. Please help me to know that we can always trust in You, dear Lord.

Prayer 56

Exodus 13–14

When things are going badly, it often seems there is no way out. That's when we need to be reminded that You are with us. Moses called to You when the Israelites were afraid that Pharaoh would catch them.

You let Moses know that You had the power to get them out of trouble. No problem is too big for You, dear God. I will trust You to make things right.

Prayer 57

Exodus 14–15

Thank You for Your many miracles, dear Lord! They come in all sizes—big and small. It's awesome to think of the sea opening up so people could walk through it. And it's amazing when a baby is born and a new life comes into the world. We are surrounded by Your miracles, dear God! Please help me to appreciate all You do for us every day.

Prayer 58

Exodus 15–16

On the first day of each week we gather together to worship You, dear God. We thank You for this day of rest. Even in Bible times, it was important to keep one day holy. When they were in the desert, Moses and Aaron told the people You would not send food to them on the Sabbath. It was more important to rest and to worship than to gather food. I pray that You will help us to remember that this day is special. Let us spend it thinking of You and all the many good things You have done for us.

Prayer 59

Exodus 17

Dear Lord, I don't always want to do what my parents or teachers say. Sometimes I'm hungry or tired or thirsty, and I start to complain. Moses' people were like this, even though he had given them what they needed so many times. I hope I can be grateful for what I have and trust that things will work out okay, even if it seems to take a long time. Lord, help me to be grateful for all that I have.

Prayer 60

Exodus 17

Even the powerful Moses needed people sometimes, dear Lord. Once, when he was watching a battle, he held up his rod to keep the Israelites going. But he grew so tired that his arms started to come down, and the Israelites started losing the battle. His friends Aaron and Hur helped prop up his arms, though. Lord, please help me to know that it's okay to ask for help sometimes and to lean on others when I can't do everything myself.

Prayer 61

Exodus 18–19

I pray for the leaders of our country, dear God. We learn in school that there are many leaders. Our city mayor, state representatives, and our president have to make important decisions every day. Even Moses in his time knew that to rule well he needed advice from others. Bless our leaders, Lord, and help them to do their jobs well.

Prayer 62

Exodus 19–20

Help me to follow Your commandments, dear Lord. Help me to put You first in my life. That's what the first of the Ten Commandments You gave Moses says. God, I pray that You will keep me close to You and that I will honor You by keeping Your rules.

Prayer 63

Exodus 20

Dear God, I know that if I follow Your commandments, I will get along better with others. If I lie or steal something from someone, it hurts them—and it hurts me too. If I keep Your laws, I will be a happier person in a happier world. Dear Lord, please help keep me strong when I'm faced with temptations.

Prayer 64

Exodus 21–24

You make promises to us, dear Lord, and sometimes You ask us to make promises to You. In the agreement You gave Moses, You shared all the many things You expect us to do—to love our friends, relatives, and neighbors and to treat them right. I pray that if I make a promise to You, I will keep it the same way You keep Your promises to us.

Prayer 65

Exodus 25–31

The church buildings where we worship You are special places, dear Lord. When You guided Moses and the Israelites in how to build their tabernacle, You were letting them know it was time to have a more formal place to gather together and worship You. Even though that tabernacle was a tent that could be packed up and moved, a lot of teamwork and sharing went into its making, which made it meaningful in Your eyes. When we're asked to help out, like painting or picking up litter around our church building, remind us of how important it is that we all pitch in to help. Dear Lord, please help me to remember how very special my church is.

Prayer 66

Exodus 32

You are the only living God, O Lord. When people worship other things like money or power, they are trusting in something that can go away as quickly as it came. Moses knew this, and he was very angry when he saw his people worshiping the golden calf. Moses had told his people to put their trust in You, but they were too impatient. Sometimes we must not be so quick to give up hope and faith. I pray that I always put my trust in You and know that You will always be there for me.

Prayer 67

Exodus 33–34

It's great to have really good friends, dear Lord. My friends stick by me in good times and in bad. This is called loyalty. Moses was very loyal to the Israelites, even though they disobeyed You. Again and again he asked for Your forgiveness for his people, Lord, and You gave it to them. Thank You for being such a just and loving God.

Prayer 68

Exodus 35–40

Sometimes You give us signs or signals that show us what we should do. They aren't always as clear as the moving cloud of Moses' time. Sometimes something inside me warns me when I'm about to make a mistake. My mom told me this is my conscience. Please help me to listen to my conscience and to obey what it tells me, dear Lord.

Prayer 69

Leviticus 11–25

The wonderful food I eat every day is a sign of Your great love for us, dear God. During Moses' time, You gave the Israelites food and in return asked that they remember You at special times each year and in special ways. You have always provided us with plenty to eat, and for that I thank You. Dear Lord, when I eat, I pray that I should show my gratitude by saying a blessing. Here is one:

Dear heavenly Father, please bless this food we are about to eat. We pray that it will help us to grow and to be strong. Bless everyone at our table. Keep us safe from harm so that we may do Your will. Thank You for this food and for Your blessings, dear Lord. Amen.

Prayer 70

Numbers 11–12

You have done so many good things for me, dear God. I can't even count them all! Moses knew this, too. That is why he was so unhappy with the Israelites when they kept complaining. You gave them so much, and they still weren't happy. Please help me to remember Your blessings when I start to complain. I have so much to be thankful for, dear Lord.

Prayer 71

Numbers 13–14

Moses' spies who went into Canaan should have trusted You no matter how big and strong the Canaanites were because You had said that one day that land would belong to the Israelites. It is easy to get discouraged because we can only see what is happening right now. If things are bad at this moment, we're afraid they won't get better. You know everything to come, dear Lord. I pray that You will help those who are worried see that things will work out for the best.

Prayer 72

Numbers 16–17

Help me to see that I should follow You instead of someone who just thinks he's big and powerful. Moses had done many wonderful things for his people, but they could not wait to see what would happen next. When Korah came along and said he was taking over, the people didn't trust in Moses' leadership. But You showed them You were the most powerful of all, God. We need to pray every day that You will show us what we should do. I will pray and listen for Your answer, Lord.

Prayer 73

Numbers 20

Everyone makes mistakes. Even Moses got upset and disobeyed You. You had told him to speak to a rock and the rock would pour out water for the people, who were thirsty. But Moses was growing angry from hearing so much complaining, so he hit the stone instead. When I make a mistake, please help me to admit it. Then I can receive Your forgiveness, dear Father.

Prayer 74

Numbers 21

Your healing power is so great, Heavenly Father. You even helped the Israelites get well after they had been bitten by snakes. We are thankful for the doctors who help us get well. Thank You for helping them. I pray that all those who are hurt and sick receive Your mercy, dear Lord. And please bless the doctors and nurses who look after us.

Prayer 75

Numbers 22–24

Angels don't always look like they do on Christmas trees. You sent Balaam an angel that only Balaam's donkey could see. When the animal spoke, You then let Balaam see the angel. It feels good to know that Your angels are around us. Thank You for sending angels to give us messages, dear God.

Prayer 76

Numbers 25–36

Our cities can be dangerous places, dear Lord. We hear about crime and about people doing bad things to each other. I wish we could have cities of safety—the kind You made for Moses' people. Murderers were not allowed in those cities because they had broken one of Your commandments. I pray for the people of our cities and towns, dear Lord. Keep them safe from harm.

Prayer 77

Deuteronomy

I don't like to be punished for something I've done. Yet I know that if I always get away with bad things, I might get the idea that it's okay to do them. Moses did many great deeds for You, Lord, but he was wrong when he disobeyed You in front of the people. Punishment reminds us that it is not okay to do wrong. Dear Lord, I pray that I learn to listen to Your rules and obey them and understand that You only ask us to do things for a reason.

Prayer 78

Joshua 1

Please help me to be brave, dear Lord, just as You helped Joshua. He must have felt so very alone without Moses and Aaron, but

You told him You would stay by his side. Whether I'm sticking up for myself against a bully or getting a shot at the doctor's office, stay by my side, Heavenly Father. Give me the strength I need as I go through life.

Prayer 79

Joshua 2

Sometimes it's hard to know what is right. Rahab must have been a very brave woman to go against her king's orders to help Joshua's spies. But she knew that You are a powerful God and that You would save her. Please help me to know whose orders to follow. Sometimes at school I get many different signals from teachers and friends. Please help me to listen closely to Your messages so I know what to do, dear Father.

Prayer 80

Joshua 3–4

The rivers and seas of this world are very important, dear God. They give us water and help people get from one place to another—even though they don't dry up so we can cross them as Joshua did when he crossed into the Promised Land! Help us to keep our lakes and oceans clean, dear God. Bless the fish and animals that live in them.

Prayer 81

Joshua 5–6

Dear Lord, in the old days, people built walls around their cities to protect them. Sometimes people build pretend walls around themselves to keep others out. Knock down our barriers from each other, dear Lord, just as You did when You knocked down the walls of Jericho. I pray

that You come inside our hearts. Please give
us the comfort we need, and show us how
to ask for help from our friends and family
when we need it. And please help me to
know when others are reaching out to me,
Lord, even if they have trouble saying it.

Prayer 82

Joshua 7

There are lots of kids who play on our
team, dear Lord. Each one plays a different
position. If we all play fairly, we have a
good chance of winning. But if one player
cheats or plays too rough, we might lose.
Joshua's army lost the battle at Ai because
some of his men had stolen things from
Jericho after a battle. They won at Jericho,
but they did not win nicely. This made You
angry, Lord, and You didn't stand beside
them in the next battle. Please help each of
us to remember how important it is to obey
You, dear God.

Prayer 83

Joshua 9

Sometimes I think I know everything, Lord. If my parents tell me to do something and I don't see the point of it right away, I don't always do what they say. Other times I forget their warnings or my own common sense. Even though You told him not to, Joshua made a peace treaty with the Gibeonites because he didn't recognize them in their disguises. He should have trusted in You to reveal them for what they were. I know it is so important to do what I've been told and to ask Your advice every day in prayer. You alone know what really is best for us, dear God.

Prayer 84

Joshua 10

When I read about how You made the sun stop in the sky over Gibeon so Joshua could win his battle, I see how powerful You are, dear God! I can count on You to help me with any problem I have. Lord, help me think of the great things You've done whenever I start to doubt You.

Prayer 85

Joshua 13–22

The Israelites trusted in You, dear Lord, and You brought them to the Promised Land just as You said. I, too, will trust You to look after me throughout my life.

Prayer 86

Joshua 24

We worship only You, dear Lord. If we worship You, we don't need to worship anything else. Some people say they worship movie stars or sports heroes. We may look up to other people, but You are our one true God. You are the one who made us. Joshua knew this. He wrote a covenant on a stone and left it with his people, so they would always remember the agreement they made to worship only You. When I worship, help me to remember never to put anyone else before my love for You, dear Lord.

Prayer 87

Judges 1–2

If I am with friends who try to get me to do something wrong, help me to say no, dear Lord. They might say, "You won't get in trouble" or "Everyone else is doing it." They're only saying that to get me to do what they want. After Joshua died, the people started to follow the Canaanites and do all the bad things they were doing. But You forgave them, God, when they were sorry. I pray You will help me to be strong when I am tempted to do wrong.

Prayer 88

Judges 3

Please help the police officers and judges who enforce our laws, dear God. Police officers have a dangerous job. Judges have to decide who is guilty or who is innocent. Even in the time of the great judges You sent to help keep the laws after Joshua died, the people kept doing wrong over and over again. I pray that our law enforcers will be fair, but also that people learn right from wrong so they don't keep breaking rules.

Prayer 89

Judges 4–5

Men and women need to help each other, dear Lord. On television I see husbands and wives fighting with each other. Some of my friends' parents are divorced. I pray that grownups will learn to get along and to be kind to one another. In the Bible, Judge Deborah and Barak helped each other fight Sisera's army. This is a good example of men and women working together. Dear Lord, help us to respect each other for what we do, not what we are.

Prayer 90

Judges 6

We don't have to be the smartest or the strongest ones to be called by You, dear Lord. Gideon told You he was just a poor farm boy. But You sent an angel to tell him that he could be a good leader and that You would stay by his side. People who are weak or poor are just as important in Your eyes as the strong. You know if we have goodness in our hearts. Dear Lord, thank You for loving the "little" people in life.

Prayer 91

Judges 6

When You show us Your great power, Lord, it helps give us courage. Gideon must have felt very scared to take on the Midianites. But when You showed him what You could do through Your angel, he knew You were with him. It gave Gideon the strength to destroy the enemy's false god, Baal, even though he knew it would get him into trouble. Please help me to stand up for what I know is right, even when it isn't easy.

Prayer 92

Judges 7

Violence is such a terrible thing, dear Lord. It is all around us—on the news, on television, and in the streets. Sometimes I may feel as if I have to fight, but there are other ways I can deal with my problems. Gideon outsmarted his enemies. That's one way to deal with them. Another way is to talk things out. There are many ways to be a strong person without pushing people around! Please help me to find peaceful ways to work out my problems, dear Lord.

Prayer 93

Judges 11

Dear Lord, I may think I want to be a line leader or have the latest video game. I often want something so badly that I would do anything to get it. But if I get something dishonestly or through promises I don't plan to keep, it's just not worth it. Jephthah made hasty promises to You so he could be king, and it cost him dearly. Help me to go after what I want honestly and fairly, dear God.

Prayer 94

Judges 13

Some signs You give us are very easy to see. You let Manoah and his wife know that they would have a child by setting their sacrifice on fire. I pray that when You send me a sign—even if it isn't as easy to see—I'll know it is a message from You.

Prayer 95

Judges 14

Dear Lord, You made a man named Samson so strong he could kill a lion with his bare hands! I see a lot of strong men in the movies. Some use their strength to help people—others just want to show off. Help me to use the strength You gave me to do good things, dear Father. And I pray that I stay strong by exercising and eating good food, so I can have the energy to keep spreading Your word.

Prayer 96

Judges 14

Dear Lord, if my friend tells me the name of the boy she likes at school, I shouldn't gossip to others about her. Samson trusted his bride not to tell the bad men the answer to his riddle. But if someone tries to do something bad to me and then tells me not to tell my parents about it, I shouldn't listen to him. I hope I can tell the difference between keeping a trust and doing the right thing. Please help me to know which secrets I should keep and which ones I should tell, dear God.

Prayer 97

Judges 15

Anger can be very harmful, dear Lord. Samson was so mad that he couldn't be with his wife that he did a cruel thing to some foxes and destroyed others' property with fire. He must not have been thinking clearly at all. Suppose someone did something bad to me: maybe he borrowed my favorite toy and didn't bring it back. Then instead of telling him how it made me feel and asking for it nicely, I took something of his and broke it. That would be wrong. Before I take revenge on someone, I pray that I stop and think of a better way to handle my problem, Lord.

Prayer 98

Judges 16

Dear Lord, people will do all kinds of things to get money. Delilah, Samson's wife, was even willing to tell the Philistines the secret of Samson's strength so they could capture him in return for a large sum of money. Cheating or lying to someone so you can get money leads to trouble. Delilah let her greed get in the way of her love for her husband. Help me to find ways to earn my money honestly, dear God. I pray that I would never betray a friend, no matter what anyone offered me.

Prayer 99

Judges 16

Dear Lord, if people really love me, they want what is good for me. They don't tell me they love me to get something they want. Please lead me to the people in my life who will truly love me, Lord. And help me never to take advantage of someone's caring like Delilah did with Samson.

Prayer 100

Judges 16

You listened to Samson's prayer for strength to punish the Philistines for blinding him, dear Lord. I know You listen to my prayers too. If it is Your will, You will answer anything I ask. You may answer yes or no— or want me to wait awhile. Whatever the answer, I know it will be the best one for me. I pray that I am open to Your will, even if it doesn't match what I want.

Prayer 101

Ruth 1

Dear Lord, our family might be a mom, dad, and kids. Or we might have step-brothers and step-sisters or a grandparent living with us. Families can be very different. Ruth wanted to stay with Naomi, her mother-in-law, after her husband died. She had come to see Naomi as her family. Your family is the whole world, dear God.

Anywhere we find people who believe in You, we are surrounded by Your family. I pray that I appreciate my family and all those who have become a part of my larger family by being close to me. Please watch over those I love and keep them safe.

Prayer 102

Ruth 2

Dear Lord, if everyone took care of each other in some small way, many of the world's problems would be solved. Boaz helped Ruth and Naomi, who were hungry, when he said they could help themselves to food and drink from his fields. He was a generous man. If each one of us would give food to a hungry person or volunteer to help someone learn to read, it would make a big difference. I pray that You show me ways to help others, dear Lord. I am ready and willing to start tomorrow!

Prayer 103

Ruth 3–4

Helping people is important, dear Lord. But sometimes we forget to help those closest to us. Boaz was Ruth and Naomi's closest family. When he married Ruth, he promised to take care of her forever. In that way he was taking care of his family. My mom and dad work hard. They could use help with the house and yard work on their days off. I know I could do something helpful for my family each day, but sometimes I get distracted by other things. Dear Lord, please help me see how important it is to pitch in and do my part.

Prayer 104

1 Samuel 1

When I hear the story of Hannah and Peninnah and how Peninnah made fun of

Hannah because she had no children, I understand that Hannah must have felt very hurt. If the kids at school make fun of each other, please give me the strength to stop them, God. Their jokes may sound funny, but I bet they wouldn't think it was so funny if the joke was on them. Please help children to treat each other better, dear Lord.

Prayer 105

1 Samuel 1

Someday I will grow up and move away from my family. Though I do look forward to that day in a way, I know that these are special times too. Hannah knew that her time with Samuel wouldn't last long because she had promised he would live his life serving You. So she made the most of the time she did have with him. I thank You for my family, my friends, my school, and my teachers. Please bless the time I spend with them.

Prayer 106

1 Samuel 1–2

Hannah allowed her son to stay with the priest Eli so that he could serve You, Lord, just as she had promised. This was a great sacrifice to make, so You rewarded her with more children. In school we are rewarded for studying hard when we get good grades. At home we may get a treat, maybe a toy or an ice-cream cone. Thank You, Lord, for the many wonderful rewards we get every day.

Prayer 107

1 Samuel 3

If You speak to me through my conscience, dear Father, as You spoke to Samuel, I pray that I will listen to You and do what You tell me. I might not want to listen if You tell me not to do something that I really want to do. I pray that I follow Your guidance in all things, so that everything will turn out for the best.

Prayer 108

1 Samuel 4

Rules are for keeping us safe and for respecting what belongs to others. If I run across the street to catch my ball and I don't stop to look both ways, I might not see a car coming toward me. If I do break a rule by taking a toy that doesn't belong to me, I might forget to bring the toy back. I might even damage it. That would make the person it belongs to very sad. When the Israelites took the ark out of Shiloh, they were breaking Your rule. You had told them not to move it, God. The ark was very important to You, and it might have been destroyed by being brought into enemy lands. I pray that I will learn to follow the rules, dear God, and respect what is Yours, and what belongs to others.

Prayer 109

1 Samuel 4

You didn't make Your rules so that things would be tougher for us, dear Lord. Your rules are to make things better. The Israelites had to learn the hard way that they had done wrong. They lost many men and the ark in battle. If I follow Your rules, I can keep from making a lot of terrible mistakes. I pray to find the inner strength to avoid doing the wrong thing.

Prayer 110

1 Samuel 5–6

Dear God, help me to understand that some things are holy. In church I see the altar, the special gowns the ministers wear, and other holy things. These items are holy because each has an important meaning in Your eyes and in the eyes of the people who come to worship. The ark was more than just a set of rules. It was a holy document put in a holy case. Such things are not to be taken lightly. This ark was filled with so much power that when it was put in the same place as an idol, the idol broke into pieces. Please help me to remember things like this, so that when I am in church I can see just how important it is to treat things there with respect.

Prayer 111

1 Samuel 7–8

Before I make up my mind about something, dear Lord, I need to think about what might happen. Samuel's people said they wanted a king, but You wanted to make sure they knew just what having a king meant. I will come to You, dear God, to pray about my wishes. I may think I have all the right ideas and I don't need any help. You know what I need before I do, dear Father. I pray that I keep my heart and mind open to You every day, dear Lord.

Prayer 112

1 Samuel 9

Dear Lord, I am always amazed when I read in the Bible that You picked ordinary people to become great leaders. Saul was only a farm boy, but You chose him to be king one day. O Lord, thank You for seeing what is special in all of us and for giving us the opportunity to succeed, even if we come from humble beginnings. I pray that I learn a lesson from this story and never feel like I am not good enough to do something or be anything I set my mind to.

Prayer 113

1 Samuel 9–10

Sometimes You ask us to do things for You, dear God. We feel a tug at our hearts telling us to take on a special role at church, like Sunday School helper. It feels good to be asked to do something new. But it can be scary too. Saul was so afraid to take up the responsibility You had put on him that he hid from the people. Maybe he felt as if he was not good enough to be a leader. Help me to stand tall and do what I know is right, Lord, and what I feel called to do.

Prayer 114

1 Samuel 11

It's not right to be a bully, Lord. The Ammonites tried to frighten the Israelites in Jabesh by saying they were going to put out the right eye of every citizen. This made Saul mad, and he organized a great army to defeat them. By his courage, Saul let the Ammonites know that they couldn't just push his people around. But I know that he couldn't have done that without Your help, Lord. Good can win out over bad with You by our side, dear Father. I pray for those who are frightened by bullies who try to scare them into giving in, Lord, and I hope I never act that way.

Prayer 115

1 Samuel 13

Sometimes when we feel as if we have done something good or have found favor in Your sight, Lord, we may feel proud of ourselves. It is good to feel special, as long as we don't forget who gave us our talent or skill. We are nothing without You, Lord. Saul started out humble, but he became very proud after he became king. Dear Father, help me always to remember that You are the one to thank for all things.

Prayer 116

1 Samuel 13–14

Dear God, Jonathan defeated the Philistines because he trusted You. He did not need a big army to win. He only needed You. You have the power to do things that seem impossible to us. Dear Lord, help me to remember that I can always depend on You.

Prayer 117

1 Samuel 15–16

Dear Lord, sometimes I promise to clean my room or stop teasing my sister for a week if I can get what I want, like a new toy or a trip to the movies. But my mom is not interested in making deals. She tells me it's more important to do those things out of love than to do them in order to get something. My mom wants me to obey her, just as Samuel told Saul it was more important to obey You than to make sacrifices to You. I pray that I will do what I know is right instead of doing as I please.

Prayer 118

1 Samuel 16

Dear Lord, on television it seems as if the richest or the best-looking people get the best things in this life. You don't care what we look like, though. Just as You told Samuel, You can see what's in our hearts, not just in our faces. You picked David to be the next king even though he had many strong, handsome brothers. You give Your blessings to all those who follow You, not just to the ones who are beautiful. Thank You, Lord, for being so fair.

Prayer 119

1 Samuel 16

Dear Lord, You have blessed us with many beautiful songs. Music can soothe us and make us happy. When Saul became mean, his people knew that music might make him feel less angry. That is why David, who could play the harp so sweetly, became so important to him. I pray that all people who are sad can find some comfort in Your wonderful gifts of song and music, Lord.

Prayer 120

1 Samuel 17

Dear Lord, I have heard people say, "Might doesn't make right." Goliath must have felt that he could beat up anybody or he would not have challenged the Israelites to choose someone to fight him. He thought he was more powerful than his whole army because he was a big man. Dear Lord, help me to realize there are many other ways to be powerful besides being bigger and stronger than everybody else.

Prayer 121

1 Samuel 17

Dear God, please give me the courage to stand up for what's right, just as David did when he agreed to fight Goliath. It's easier to go along with the crowd or to hang back in the background. I pray that I won't be afraid to go against the crowd or a bully if what they're doing is wrong.

Prayer 122

1 Samuel 17

We are so thankful for Your power, dear God. You gave a little boy the power to kill a giant! If David could beat Goliath with Your help, I know I can count on You to help me too. Dear Lord, the next time I feel small and insignificant, I pray that I remember the story of David and Goliath and know that I can do great things too.

Prayer 123

1 Samuel 17–18

Dear Lord, I feel sad when a person who acts like my friend turns against me. It makes me feel bad when that happens. I wonder what I did to her to make her not like me anymore. David must have felt like this when Saul threw a spear at him. He had played the harp for Saul many times and thought he was one of the king's favorite friends. Please be there for me if I lose a friend, dear God. Help me to know that it's not always my fault if someone turns away from me. Also, let me know if I start to do this to someone else, so I can stop being mean.

Prayer 124

1 Samuel 19

Dear Lord, Jonathan, Saul's son, was brave to go against his father's wishes and help David. He was a good friend to David. If I see a friend about to get into trouble, please let me be able to warn him, Lord. He might not want to hear what I have to say, but I pray that he will listen to me and stay away from danger. I pray that I will accept the responsibility of real friendship and tell the truth if I have to.

Prayer 125

1 Samuel 20

Dear Lord, when we are at the pool or the beach, the lifeguard tells us when we should get out of the water. Sometimes she signals to other lifeguards when something dangerous is happening. Jonathan was clever to come up with a signal to alert David if Saul was trying to kill him. I pray that I will see Your danger signs, dear God. I trust You to keep me safe.

Prayer 126

1 Samuel 20

Dear Lord, Jonathan and David had become such good friends that Jonathan was very sad when he knew David had to leave and never come back. We can't always be with the ones we love. Friends move away, or family members have to go away from home. When that happens, dear Lord, I know that You will stay with me as You did with Jonathan.

Prayer 127

1 Samuel 21

Dear Lord, people think it's okay to tell a "little white lie." David thought it was all right to say he was on a secret mission from Saul so he could get some bread and Goliath's sword. He was hungry, which made it hard for him to stay honest. But still, little lies can get us in just as much trouble as big ones. The main thing is that any type of lying is wrong. Please help me to tell the truth always, dear God.

Prayer 128

1 Samuel 22

Dear Lord, David's little lie turned into a very serious lie because it caused the priests to be killed. I'm sure he didn't mean for them to get hurt. Most of the time when we lie we're doing it to keep ourselves from getting in trouble or to get something we want. We don't understand all the problems our lies can cause. This is what people mean when they talk about consequences. You understand, Lord. That's why You want us to be truthful. I pray that I will grow up to be an honest person others can trust, Lord.

Prayer 129

1 Samuel 23

Dear Lord, sometimes it's hard to know what battles or causes are worth fighting for. The reasons for arguing might not seem to be important enough, or maybe winning seems impossible. David wasn't sure if his army of six hundred men was enough to defeat the Philistines, but You helped him decide to attack. Although fighting is rarely the right way to handle something, please help me to know when I should take a stand or defend myself, dear God, I pray.

Prayer 130

1 Samuel 24

Dear Lord, David knew that Saul wanted him dead, but still he could not bring himself to hurt Saul when he had the chance. Revenge is not for us. Judgment is something for You to handle, dear Lord. If we try to get back at people, it only makes things worse. I pray that I will leave judgment in Your hands and have a forgiving heart, like David's.

Prayer 131

1 Samuel 25

Dear Lord, our kindness can sometimes make up for another's meanness. When David asked a farmer, Nabal, if he could share the harvest of his fields, Nabal showed his meanness by turning down David's request. But Nabal's wife, Abigail, wanted to make up for her husband's temper. She brought food to David and his men. If I see a big kid pushing a little kid on the playground, I can go to the little kid and ask him to come join our group. I pray that I will find many ways to show kindness, dear Lord.

Prayer 132

1 Samuel 25

God, it's really hard when someone we know and love, like a relative or friend, does something bad to someone else. Is it right to go against him? Will he still like us if we do? Nabal's wife had to make a decision whether to obey her husband or You. But she was right to feed David's men, even though her husband wanted to hurt them. Even though Nabal was her husband, You are the Heavenly Father to us all, Lord. We must do what we think is right when we see something bad about to happen to someone. Because Abigail believed in You, dear Lord, she found the courage to do a good deed. I pray that You give me the same strength if I ever have to make a tough decision like that, dear God.

Prayer 133

1 Samuel 26

I know I can be stubborn, Lord. Sometimes I have to have something repeated many times before I learn it. King Saul was like that. Even after David had spared his life, Saul still tried to harm him. Please let me learn from my mistakes, Lord, and help me to become a better person when I am confronted with goodness in others.

Prayer 134

1 Samuel 27–28

Lord, I know You are a forgiving God, but help me learn that my actions may have lasting consequences. If I yell at my parents once and say I'm sorry, they might forgive me. But if I do that every night, eventually my apologies won't mean anything. King Saul was wrong to keep chasing David for so many years. When David finally turned the Philistines against him, Saul asked Samuel's spirit for help. Samuel told Saul that You were no longer with him, Lord. We can't keep doing the wrong thing and then expect everything to turn out okay. Help me to change, Lord, and to stop doing bad things.

Prayer 135

1 Samuel 29–30

Wars are scary, Lord. Soldiers fight each other, and innocent people get killed. Wars have been going on for thousands of years, since Bible times. The Israelites were always at war. Sometimes when I read the Bible, it's hard to tell who was fighting whom. That's probably because, deep down, we are all just people, very much like one another. I pray for peace, dear Lord. Please help us to get along.

Prayer 136

1 Samuel 30

If a player has to sit on the bench during a game, he or she is still part of the team. Even if it seems as if the star players get the credit for a win, everybody who helps the team should share in the victory. David understood this when he told his warriors to share the winnings with the men who had to stay behind because they were so tired. I pray that we will all thank You for our victories, dear Lord!

Prayer 137

1 Samuel 31

Dear God, it's hard for me to understand how people could be so cruel to one another. Sometimes it's kind of fun to watch television and movie fighting. Real fighting, like in Bible times when Saul and his sons were killed by the Philistines, is scary and mean. Please help us to learn to love one another.

Prayer 138

2 Samuel 2–4

Let us not carry on our parents' or friends' fights, dear Lord. If my mom or dad or a friend from school is mad at someone, I hope I wouldn't keep the fight going just to be loyal. When Saul's son, Ish-Bosheth, tried to carry on the feud his father had had with David, he finally came to see it was no use. Holding a grudge against someone or his family is wrong. I pray that I will have the courage to stay friends with someone even if others don't think I should.

Prayer 139

2 Samuel 5–6

David and his men were able to do great things. They listened and followed what You told them, dear Father, and You helped David and his army defeat the Jebusites in Jerusalem. Jerusalem became the city of David. Then You helped David defend his city against the Philistines. You can make the impossible possible, Lord! You make me have hope in the future. Praise be to You for all You do for Your people.

Prayer 140

2 Samuel 6

There are some things that are really special to You, dear Lord. The ark of the covenant was so meaningful that no one was supposed to touch it. David traveled a great distance to bring the ark back to Jerusalem because it was so important to keep it in a special place and treat it right. The cross is another symbol of Your love for us, just as the flag is a great symbol of freedom and our love for our country. Whether they are made of gold or paper, help us to remember to treat such special things with respect, dear Lord, I pray.

Prayer 141

2 Samuel 6

We show our thanks to You in many ways, dear Lord. Sometimes we pray quietly, and sometimes we sing a joyful song. David was so happy to have been made king that he danced and sang with the people in the streets. Sometimes I feel like that too! I have so many blessings, Lord, that I can find a hundred ways to show You my thanks! I pray that I will never seem ungrateful in Your eyes.

Prayer 142

2 Samuel 7

Dear Lord, I have a lot of big ideas. I imagine I will go somewhere far away or build my own robot. My mom and dad say, "Maybe someday." When I pray to You, Lord, I think that maybe You're telling me the same thing. Someday I will grow up and do the things I dream about. Or it might even be my daughter or son who lives out my dreams. David wanted to build a lasting house for the ark. This was his big plan, but You told him the time wasn't right. You said his son would be the one to do this when he was king. Sometimes it's hard to put our dreams on hold, but with Your help, Lord, we can learn patience.

Prayer 143

2 Samuel 9

Taking care of others is important work, dear Lord. If we all treated one another as brothers and sisters instead of as enemies, the world would be a better place. David was very kind to keep his old promise to his friend Jonathan. He had told Jonathan that he would take care of his family. Even though Jonathan's father, Saul, was David's enemy, David was a forgiving person. Please help me to find ways to care for others, Lord.

Prayer 144

2 Samuel 11

Dear Lord, I may see something I want very badly, like a really great bicycle with lots of gears. But if that bike belongs to someone else and I take it, I have broken the law and Your rules too. I may be happy for a little while because I got what I wanted. But then I realize the trouble I've caused and all my happiness goes away. David never should have tried to take Bathsheba away from her husband, Uriah. He broke one of Your commandments, Lord. I pray I will be content with the many wonderful things You give me every day without wanting what other people have.

Prayer 145

2 Samuel 11

God, I know You will forgive me if I make a stupid mistake. We all do that sometimes.

But if I were to do something terrible—like hurting or killing someone—that would be going against Your most sacred laws. David sent Uriah to be killed so he could have his wife, Bathsheba. This was very bad in Your sight, Lord. Help me to understand that You made these serious rules to protect us from each other. Help me to treat others well and not be greedy.

Prayer 146

2 Samuel 11

Dear Lord, if we break a rule and nothing happens right away, we may think we have gotten away with it. But You know everything we do, Lord. You remember the good things and the bad things. David thought that if he waited for Bathsheba to get over Uriah's death, he could bring her to the palace and soon all would be forgotten. He would have what he wanted. But You never forget, God! I pray that I do what is right so that I don't offend You, Lord.

Prayer 147

2 Samuel 12

People who have a lot of power can get some crazy ideas. They think that because they are the leaders, they don't have to follow the rules anymore. Your rules are the same for everyone, dear Lord, rich and poor. When Nathan told David the story about the rich man stealing the poor man's only lamb, David was mad. At first he did not see that this is just what he had done to Uriah. This is why You had to teach David a serious lesson. Even though You forgave him for his sins, You took away his son. Please help me see that I must never use my power to steal from others, Lord.

Prayer 148

2 Samuel 12–13

Some of my friends have half- or stepbrothers and sisters, dear Lord. They play together and fuss like regular brothers and sisters. It's easy to let petty jealousy and competition get out of hand when families are all mixed together. David's sons Absalom and Amnon treated each other very badly. I pray for all families to be close and to get along with one another, dear Lord.

Prayer 149

2 Samuel 14

Dear Lord, it's hard to forgive someone if he's done something really terrible. David must have found it really hard to forgive Absalom, but he still missed him so much. I pray that with Your help, I will make the right decisions about forgiving people today and every day.

Prayer 150

2 Samuel 15

Dear Lord, when we are good to people, we expect them to treat us well in return. Sadly, that doesn't always happen. David must have been very sad when Absalom tried to take over his kingdom, especially after David had forgiven him. Please stay by my side if others turn against me, dear Lord.

Prayer 151

2 Samuel 15–16

Dear Lord, when David was being yelled at by one of Saul's men, David's helper, Hushai, thought they should kill the man for his rudeness. But David said the man was sent by You, God, to curse him for his sins. Hushai saw only one side of the story. Only You know both sides of every story, Lord. I pray that I won't be so quick to judge a situation when it is happening.

Prayer 152

2 Samuel 17

Dear Lord, it's sad that David couldn't trust his own son Absalom. Absalom should not have trusted David's man Hushai. But Absalom didn't know Hushai had been sent to spy on him. I don't always know who to trust, dear God. Even my best friend tells my secrets sometimes. I am so glad I can trust You, though. Our best advice comes from You, Heavenly Father. If we will pray to You, You will show us the answers. I will come to You with my problems, dear Lord, and I know You will help me solve them.

Prayer 153

2 Samuel 18

Running away is not a good way to solve a problem. The "easy way out" often turns out to be the hardest. Absalom didn't know David had told his men to be merciful to him. After a battle he tried to run away, but his hair got caught in a tree instead. If he had just faced up to the enemy, he would have been much better off. Please help me to face up to my problems, dear Lord. With Your help things will get better.

Prayer 154

2 Samuel 18

Help me to listen to You and follow You every day, dear Lord. Listening is hard for me. Dad says the words "go in one ear and out the other." This is what happened to Joab when a soldier tried to tell him that he was supposed to let Absalom live. Please let Your words stay with me, O Lord, I pray.

Prayer 155

2 Samuel 18–19

Dear Lord, parents love their children, even if they don't always get along with them. The same goes for children. David was heartbroken when he heard of Absalom's death, even though Absalom had tried to take his throne. Please help us to be careful of what we say and do to our loved ones, dear God. Family is family, no matter what happens. I pray that I treat them with all the love and respect they deserve, just like the Bible tells me.

Prayer 156

1 Kings 1

Plans can change very quickly, dear Lord. I might think that I was going to be invited to a friend's birthday party, but I shouldn't start planning to go until I get the invitation. Lord, You have a plan that happens no matter what we think or do. David's son Adonijah thought he was going to be king, and he started making plans for his crowning ceremony. He was acting too soon, though, because You knew Solomon was going to be the next king after David. I will trust You no matter what happens.

Prayer 157

1 Kings 1–2

Dear God, Adonijah wanted to marry Abishag. Abishag had been King David's nurse before David died. This marriage would have helped Adonijah become king, but God, You had already chosen Solomon to be the next king. Dear Lord, I don't ever want to go against Your wishes. Help me to be happy with the way things are and are meant to be.

Prayer 158

1 Kings 3

Solomon acted very cleverly when he settled the argument between the two mothers who both claimed a baby was theirs. When he suggested they cut the baby in half, he never meant for that to happen. He just wanted to see which mother would cry out because he knew the woman who fought to protect the child at all costs was the real mother. My mom and dad want to protect me. That's why they won't let me play in the street or stay out late. Though I might wish I could do more, please help me to respect their wishes. Your rules are to protect us, too, Lord. I am thankful to You and to my parents for keeping me safe.

Prayer 159

1 Kings 5, 6, 8

Dear Lord, I'm not always ready when it's time to go to church. I may be too sleepy or too busy playing a game. Then I remember that I'm going to visit with You, dear God. Help me to remember how thankful the people were in King Solomon's time when he finished the great temple to hold the ark of the covenant. It took seven years to build the temple, but it was worth the wait. I should be grateful that I have a wonderful place to worship You. I pray that I never take Your house for granted.

Prayer 160

1 Kings 7, 9, 10

Dear Lord, it would be wonderful to be as wise as King Solomon. He knew so much! But he didn't begin that way. Once he was my age. It took Your help, God, and years of experience for him to become so smart. Help me to study hard in school, dear Lord. I pray that I will always do my best.

Prayer 161

1 Kings 11

Being with the wrong crowd can get me into trouble. Many children do bad things, even if they really don't want to, just because the rest of the gang is doing it. Solomon was such a wise person, but even he started worshiping idols because his wife did. Solomon could have been a great king, but he broke Your commandments, God. Please help me to stay away from the wrong crowd.

Prayer 162

1 Kings 11–12

Dear Lord, during King Solomon's reign he had his people build the temple to house the ark of the covenant. It took many long years of hard work. At the time, the people probably didn't complain. But after Solomon died and Rehoboam took over, they wanted to make sure the next king treated them better. In school I expect to do hard work, Lord. I read about King Rehoboam and how he vowed to be even harder on the people than his father had been. It reminded me of a teacher I had who always made us be quiet and sit still. We never felt like we did a good job, and it was very tiring. Most of the time, if we trust people, they will treat us fairly in return. Help us to treat each other fairly, dear God.

Prayer 163

1 Kings 12

Dear Lord, King Rehoboam wanted to find out what kind of ruler he should be. First, he went to some older men. They told him that if he treated the people fairly, he would win their loyalty for life. Then he asked some younger men. These men told him he should be twice as hard on the people so he would not seem weak. Rehoboam should have listened to the older men. They were wise and knew from experience what was right. So many times I see children and other people making fun of older people because they have trouble walking or they sound funny. But we should respect older people. They know a lot more than we do! Dear Lord, please help me to appreciate my grandparents and other older people, and to stand up to those who treat older citizens badly. I know You would want me to do this, Lord.

Prayer 164

1 Kings 12

Dear Lord, it's easy to worship You when our parents take us to church and follow Your rules. If we had a president or a parent who worshiped false gods and didn't let us worship You, it would be more difficult.

The people of Israel didn't have a great choice when it came to leaders: Rehoboam had threatened to work them hard, and Jeroboam worshiped golden calves. Please be with all of those who have to struggle to keep their faith.

Prayer 165

1 Kings 13

Dear Lord, it's exciting to hear about the prophets. They brought messages from You to Your people, Lord. Whenever they were around, it seemed as if amazing things happened. One prophet came to the altar of Jeroboam's golden calves. He told the idol worshipers that You would make the altar split in two, spilling its ashes. Jeroboam tried to stop this, but his arm wouldn't move! You had sent Jeroboam a strong message. Lord, when people at church or others try to tell me how I should act or what You want me to do, please help me to listen with respect and not be stubborn.

Prayer 166

1 Kings 13

Lord, please help me to obey my parents' rules about strangers. My parents and teachers have told me never to talk to or go off with a stranger, even if that person says he is a friend or acts nice to me. This is a very important rule! When the prophet who had split Jeroboam's altar in two met someone else who said he was a prophet, he went with him, even though You had told him to go straight home. The stranger said that You had sent him to take the first prophet home. The first prophet should have listened to You, Lord, and not gone off with a stranger, because it cost him his life. If I say I'm going to do something risky "just this once, because it's probably okay," remind me, Lord, that once is all it takes to get into trouble.

Prayer 167

1 Kings 14

Sometimes when I do something wrong, I think when I'm punished I won't hear about it again. But I need to know that my actions have consequences that may happen long after I've disobeyed. Jeroboam and his wife were worried about their son, who became very sick. Jeroboam was being punished for worshiping false gods. He should have heard Your warnings from the prophet and others long before, but he kept up his bad ways. It's hard when we are punished, dear Father, but like a good parent You have to be very strict sometimes so we don't sin again. I pray that You watch over me always and help me to understand.

Prayer 168

1 Kings 15–16

The kings of Bible times, such as Abijam, leader of Judah, had a hard time obeying You, dear God. When they disobeyed, they caused problems for themselves and for their country. Because they set a bad example for their people, the Israelites continued to do bad things such as worship idols. This is like in school, when the younger children look up to me. If I'm rude or refuse to come in when the teacher calls me in from recess, they might see what I do and try to do those things themselves. Lord, help me to think about how my behavior affects others before I do bad things.

Prayer 169

1 Kings 16

This would be a terrible place without Your laws, Heavenly Father. Everyone would do anything they pleased, hurting anybody who got in their way. This was the way it was in Samaria, under the leadership of Omri and Ahab. Thank You, Lord, for giving us rules to live by.

Prayer 170

1 Kings 17

I admit I don't think about the wheat that grows in the fields, dear Lord. The bread on our table comes from the wheat, though, and I sure pay attention to that! Today we have so much food. I can get anything I want at the school cafeteria. At home I've got lots of fruit, snacks, and good things to eat. Sometimes I take all that food for granted. The people of Samaria probably did, too. But because they worshiped false idols, You sent them a warning about their behavior by drying up the land so the grain wouldn't grow. You showed Your appreciation for Your prophet Elijah by giving him food and water when everyone else had trouble getting any. I'm sure Elijah appreciated every bite and every sip! Next time I go to the grocery store and see an entire aisle filled with all kinds of food, I hope I thank You, Father, for Your many blessings.

Prayer 171

1 Kings 17–18

Sometimes we have to take a chance and help people. The widow in Samaria who gave Elijah some of her food and water must have wondered if she would have enough for herself and her family. She might have worried that her own supplies would dry up. It would have been easy for her to tell Elijah to go away. But she had a feeling that You had sent him, Lord, so she shared with him what she had. You rewarded her when You brought her son back to life after he had died! When she saw that miracle, she knew she had done the right thing. I hope that I can be generous to others every day, Lord—even if I don't see a miracle happen. You put us on this earth together to take care of each other. You answer our prayers in wonderful ways, dear God. We can count on You to look after our every need.

Prayer 172

1 Kings 18

Dear Lord, we are so quick to blame others when things go wrong. We tattle and point fingers at each other. "She did it," we'll say. King Ahab blamed Elijah for the terrible drought. Elijah was not the cause of it. As Your prophet, he just brought the news to the people that the drought would happen because they had disobeyed. Next time, God, I pray that I look at myself before I start blaming someone else.

Prayer 173

1 Kings 18

It's hard to know which kids to hang out with, Lord. I'm tempted to go with the big, popular crowd sometimes, even when I really like children who aren't in that crowd. I figure just because a lot of people think a certain way, I should too. Elijah was one prophet of God against 450 prophets of Baal, a false god. He must have felt very alone, but he knew he worshiped the only true God. He made that huge group of prophets gather at both altars, Lord, so he could show them whose god was the one and only God. He was sure that You would be with him when the time came, Lord. I pray that I will always know without a doubt that You are with me. Please help me to follow You in good times and in bad.

Prayer 174

1 Kings 18

When I read the story of Elijah at the altar of Baal, I am sure You are the one true God. Elijah watched Ahab's people call and call to their false god, Baal. He laughed and told them their god must be asleep. No all-powerful god who really cares about people would fail to answer when they cry out. You're never "asleep" when I need You, dear God. No matter what time of the night or day, I know I can count on You to hear me. Thank You, Lord.

Prayer 175

1 Kings 18

Even though You have to teach us hard lessons, Lord, You are also very forgiving. After You set Ahab's altar on fire so that the false prophets could see Your power, You sent a message through Elijah that the rains would come again. You knew the people had been punished enough. Thank You for Your generosity, Lord. Please help me to be as forgiving of others as You have been to me.

Prayer 176

1 Kings 19

Not everyone is happy about Your power, dear Lord. Some people wish they had as much power as You do. Queen Jezebel, Ahab's wife, was one of those people. She would not listen when her husband told her of the powerful things You had done, Lord.

She was an angry and cruel woman. She threatened to kill Elijah. Protect us from people, Father, who refuse to be humbled by Your great power. When most people have too much power, they use it to do bad things. I know You are the only one who can handle so much power. Thank You, Lord, for using Your power for good.

Prayer 177

1 Kings 19

I get disappointed if my best friends don't eat lunch with me every day, even though I know they have other friends they want to be with and other things they have to do. When Elijah journeyed to Mount Horeb, he waited and waited for You to join him, as You had done so many times. He might have been disappointed that You didn't come right away, but he waited patiently. Soon, You spoke to him and told him what to do. You take care of all of us, Lord.

Please help me wait calmly when my friends can't spend all of their time with me. I know that if I'm patient, like Elijah, they'll come back.

Prayer 178

1 Kings 20

The bullies in my school think they can march in and take whatever they want, Lord. They are like Ben-hadad, king of Syria. Ben-hadad ordered King Ahab to give him all of his women, children, silver, and gold. He thought he could get away with this because he had a bigger army. When Ahab refused, Ben-hadad threatened to turn Samaria into a pile of dust. There are better ways to be "big." The biggest people of all have big hearts. Lord, I pray You will look out for all of us "little guys." Help us to stand up for what's right.

Prayer 179

1 Kings 20

With Your help, Lord, a small group can do great things. Ben-hadad had the bigger army, but Ahab had You on his side. He fought Ben-hadad and won! Impossible things become possible with Your help. Miracles do happen! Thank You, Heavenly Father, for sending us so many blessings.

Prayer 180

1 Kings 21

Dear Lord, sometimes I'm like King Ahab. He got so upset when one of his farmers, Naboth, wouldn't give him his vineyards that he refused to eat. I get so mad that I lose my appetite too. Sometimes I yell and slam doors. It doesn't do any good to get angry though. When I'm upset, I need to come to You, Lord. I can read a story in the Bible that will help me understand what is happening in my life.

Prayer 181

1 Kings 21

Dear Lord, Jezebel did some bad things. She signed Ahab's name on an order to kill Naboth so they could have his land. Jezebel and Ahab found out that tricking people to get what they wanted would not make them happy. You were very angry at Ahab, God, but You listened when he felt sad and fasted for many days. It is very important to admit when we have done wrong. I pray I can tell my parents, teachers, or friends I'm sorry when I've wronged them. It's just the right thing to do!

Prayer 182

1 Kings 22

Dear Lord, I know I shouldn't just tell people what they want to hear. Ahab's prophets told him to attack the land of

Ramoth, which belonged to the Israelites. But Jehoshaphat knew they should ask Your prophets what to do, Lord. Your prophets would tell them the right thing to do. If my friend asks me, "What would you think if I told you I took this toy from the store without paying," I would tell her that she should return the toy right away. She might get mad, but someday she would understand that I was being a real friend. I pray that I find the strength to stand up for what is right.

Prayer 183

1 Kings 22

It's easy to hang around people who always have good things to say about me. But I know a good friend, a real friend, doesn't always tell me what I want to hear. Sometimes my friends try to tell me something I'm doing wrong—like when I'm being mean or selfish. It might make me mad at first, but I know they're only trying to help me. Ahab didn't want to listen to what Your prophet Micaiah had to say. Ahab said that Micaiah usually had bad things to say about him. But Micaiah was just sending warnings from You, God, of things Ahab should or shouldn't do. Lord, please give me the strength to be honest with my friends when they need me to be and to listen when they are giving me advice.

Prayer 184

1 Kings 22–2 Kings 1

Dear Lord, When Elijah told King Ahaziah he'd be punished for worshiping idols, the king paid no attention. He wanted to do the same things he had always done. Help us listen to You, dear Father. You know what is good for us.

Prayer 185

2 Kings 2

Dear Lord, the story of how Your great prophet, Elijah, rose to heaven and turned over his power of prophecy to his helper Elisha is amazing. Fiery chariots and rivers that part in the middle—that's awesome! Then I look outside at the sunrise and the baby birds that just hatched in the nest, and I know Your miracles are all around us, dear God.

Prayer 186

2 Kings 2

Dear Lord, when someone is called to heaven it's not always easy for those left behind to understand why it had to happen. When Elijah went to heaven, the people refused to believe he was really gone. Elisha tried to tell them not to look for Elijah because he wasn't coming back. Death is hard to accept, Lord. Please be with those who have lost a loved one and comfort them in their pain.

Prayer 187

2 Kings 3

Dear God, the new king, Jehoram, put the statue of the god Baal away so people would stop worshiping it. There is a lesson in this story for me: Maybe if I put away some things that keep me from You, Lord, it would make it easier for me to follow You. I will try to get rid of bad habits, like playing video games when I should be studying or helping my mom. Please help me be strong when I am tempted to do wrong, O Lord, I pray.

Prayer 188

2 Kings 3

Dear Lord, the story of the Moabites reminds me of a tale about a bird that flew into a window one day. He had seen the reflection of the sky in the glass and thought he could keep on flying, but he crashed instead. Elisha had told King Jehoram's soldiers to dig ditches in the valley and they would beat the Moabites. That night rains filled the ditches with water. When the Moabites saw the rising sun reflected in the rain-filled ditches, they thought they were seeing the blood from the Israelites' fighting, so they attacked. Like the bird seeing the sky in the window, the Moabites were only seeing an illusion, not what was real. They were too excited about beating the Israelites. Help me to slow down and ask for Your direction, Lord.

Prayer 189

2 Kings 4

You provide for us in ways we can't even imagine, Lord. So many little blessings come into our lives every day. We can't even imagine what it would be like to have nothing, like the widow who had only one jar of oil. In Bible times oil was used for everything—cooking, lighting a house, and more. To run out of oil meant no food or light. But through You, Elisha performed a miracle! He told the widow to take her little pot of oil and pour it into some empty pots. The pot kept filling the others, on and on! She had enough to take care of her family and even some to sell so she could repay her debts. Let us take time to be thankful for Your blessings.

Prayer 190

2 Kings 4

Dear Lord, the small things we do each day for others help us out too. An older person smiles when I open the door for her. My dad says, "Thanks," when I hand him the tool he wanted. When Elisha was traveling around doing Your work, Lord, a kind woman even built a room for him in her house just so he would have a place to stay! These things make people feel good inside. I know I'm helping make the world a better place when I do Your will. I pray that You show me ways I can do things for others every day.

Prayer 191

2 Kings 4

Dear Lord, it's scary when terrible things happen. The woman who had helped Elisha had a son, but when he was still a boy, he died suddenly. How awful that must have been for her! She knew she had to run for help to "the man of God." Many of us don't come to You unless we have a problem, Lord. It's good to know You are always there. I will call for You in bad times and say my prayers of thanks in the good times.

Prayer 192

2 Kings 4

Dear Lord, our prayers are not always answered right away. We might think You didn't hear us or we didn't pray long enough. Even though the Shunammite woman did everything Elisha told her, her dead son did not come back to life right away. You do hear us, though, Lord. You will answer our prayers when the time is right.

Prayer 193

2 Kings 4

Elisha was a true prophet, Lord. He did many great things for many people. But even he couldn't bring the woman's son back to life without Your help. At first he told the woman to lay his staff on the boy, but that didn't work. Then Elisha prayed to You, Lord. After that, when Elisha put his arms around the boy, he came back to life! Even though You might perform miracles through other people, only You can really make them happen. I pray that I will spread the news of Your glory to others, Lord.

Prayer 194

2 Kings 4

Elisha continued doing Your work, Lord. Once, when he was eating with some people, they discovered that the stew they had made from a gourd was poisoned. Elisha took some meal and stirred it into the stew. Then it was safe to eat! I know Your miracles were not done as showy tricks, Lord.

The people of Elisha's day were doubtful and worshiped many false gods. You were showing them that the messengers You were sending were not ordinary people. When miracles happened, the people knew that Your spirit was near. Today, I don't have to see miracles happen to know You are with me, Lord. You are everywhere, and I love You.

Prayer 195

2 Kings 5

You offer Your help to us all, dear Father! The highest ruler or the poorest child can come to You. A good man named Naaman, who had leprosy, heard of Elisha's healing powers and asked to see him. The king of Israel turned him away, but Elisha asked that Naaman be brought before him anyway. Elisha knew that You wouldn't want him to take sides, God. Your love is great enough to take care of us all.

Prayer 196

2 Kings 5

We don't have to put on a big show or climb mountains to receive Your blessing, Lord. A single prayer or one good deed can be all You ask of us. Naaman was doubtful at first when he heard that Elijah just wanted him to bathe in the Jordan River. He did not believe that was enough to cure him. It seemed too easy. But Your spirit is all around us, Lord. You don't have to answer our prayers in a big, booming voice. Sometimes just my father's pat on the back or a call from a friend lets me know my prayers have been answered. Show me the small ways I can do Your will, Lord.

Prayer 197

2 Kings 5

Elisha didn't want to take gifts from Naaman for doing Your work, dear God. He was happy that You helped him do miracles. He understood that it was Your power, not his, that was behind them. If we could all be happy with what we have instead of trying to get more, we could live in peace with one another. I pray that I learn to be satisfied with what I have and that I give You the credit for all the good things I can do, O Lord.

Prayer 198

2 Kings 5

Dear Lord, when I go to the grocery store with my mother or father, I see so many things I would like to have. Ice cream, cereal, candy, and toys sit on the shelves waiting for me to take them home. But I know I can't get something every time I go to the store. I don't always deserve a treat, and my mother knows what is best for me. Gehazi didn't obey Elisha when he went after Naaman to get some gifts from him. I know that if I'm good, my mother will let me get something every now and then. I don't have to be sneaky about it. Thank You, Lord, for the treats I do get, and help me to accept the situation when I don't get what I want.

Prayer 199

2 Kings 6

We know we are supposed to treat our friends fairly, dear Lord. Does that mean we have to treat the boys who tease us on the bus fairly too? When the Syrians started fighting with the Israelites again, Elisha warned the Israelites of the Syrians' plans. The Syrian king sent an army to capture Elisha, but Elisha prayed that the soldiers would be blind to everything around them. You answered his prayer, Lord, and the soldiers were led into the Israelites' camp. The Israelite king wanted to kill them, but Elisha said they should be let go. He knew that Your will was to be merciful, Lord. Help me to be fair to everyone.

Prayer 200

2 Kings 6–7

Dear Lord, every winter I think spring
will never get here. I can't wait until I see
the green leaves and the daffodils. Even
during the coldest times, I believe in the
promise of spring to come. Help me to be
patient while I wait for things to get better.
The people of Samaria had faith that the
food You promised would arrive, even
though it seemed impossible. Thank You
for being constant like the seasons, dear
Lord. You won't let us down.

Prayer 201

2 Kings 7

Things don't always go my way, dear Lord.
I may not get the exact toy I want for my
birthday. Sometimes my teacher doesn't give
me the class job I want. Please help me not
to be discouraged. Although the sick and
hungry men were not allowed into the city

of Samaria, You gave them everything they needed. When I feel that the world has let me down, I can turn to You, dear Father. You will welcome me with open arms!

Prayer 202

2 Kings 7

Dear Lord, the lepers who gathered outside Samaria were wise to share their new good fortune with other people. Just as Elisha had predicted, there was enough food for everyone. The sick men knew that keeping things all for themselves would make them feel lonely and selfish. It makes all of us happy when we share what we have with others. I pray that I will not try to keep everything for myself when I get good things, Lord.

Prayer 203

2 Kings 8

Dear Lord, the prophets of the Bible brought both good and bad news to the people. It was easy to tell the good things that made everyone happy. It was not as easy to tell bad news—or to hear it either. Elisha did not want to let the king of Syria know that the king would die and be replaced with an evil man. Please be with us if bad news comes, dear Lord.

Prayer 204

2 Kings 9

Dear Lord, our leaders are chosen much differently from those in Bible times. You told Elisha who would be the next king of Israel. We vote for the candidate who will do the best job. When I'm old enough to vote, I pray that You will guide me to make the best choice.

Prayer 205

2 Kings 9

Dear Lord, we want peace to come, yet we still fight. Just as in Bible times, our leaders often struggle for power. Just like the Israelites and all their enemies, it seems as though the world will never be completely at peace. We want You to come into our lives, dear Lord, yet we push You out when we do not get along with each other. Teach us to be peaceful, Lord.

Prayer 206

2 Kings 9

Dear Lord, Jezebel reminds me of the evil queens in the fairy tales I read. She didn't care about anyone but herself. She thought the rules were for everyone else. The real Jezebel and the storybook queens had to pay for the evil things they did. Protect us, Lord, from people who make bad choices.

Prayer 207

2 Kings 11

Wow! Imagine being a king when you're only seven years old—like Joash! That must have been quite a job for such a little boy. But Joash had You to guide him, Lord. He knew he could trust You to help him lead the country. Help me to remember that if I trust in Your guidance, I can do great things even though I'm only a child. I pray that I remember stories about children like Joash and keep on dreaming big dreams, dear God.

Prayer 208

2 Chronicles 23–24

A boy-king was able to bring the people back to You, dear Lord. But he knew that he would need someone experienced to guide him, so the priest Jehoiada stayed by his side. Even though children are just as important as adults, they should understand that adults have learned a lot from their experiences. I pray that I will listen to my parents, teachers, grandparents, and others who have lived through many of the things I will live through and know how to guide me.

Prayer 209

2 Chronicles 24

Dear Lord, great things can happen if people work together. Under the guidance of King Joash, everyone helped in whatever way they could to make repairs on their temple. In my school, we each bring a can of food at Thanksgiving. When we put it all together, many families can have a holiday meal. Each one of us can help make a big difference, Lord.

Prayer 210

2 Chronicles 24

Dear Lord, teamwork is important. Members of the team count on one another to get the job done. When Jehoiada died, King Joash lost a good friend who had helped him to be strong. Joash started to make bad decisions, even though others wanted to help him do the right thing. Please help us to see how important it is to stick together, dear Lord. Help me to be there when someone is counting on me.

Prayer 211

2 Chronicles 25

Dear Lord, there's a saying that goes, "Seeing is believing." It's simple to believe in something if you can see it and touch it. Faith is about believing in things you can't always see or feel. King Amaziah didn't think his army could win in battle. He wanted to hire extra soldiers. Instead, he listened to the prophet's message and went into battle without the extra help. You were all the extra help he needed! Please help our faith in You grow stronger every day, dear Lord.

Prayer 212

2 Chronicles 25

Dear Lord, boasting to people about how great we are won't win us any friends. Amaziah lost his kingdom because he believed that he could not be beaten. If we do the right things and treat people well, others will see how nice we are and like us for ourselves. Dear God, help me not to brag around my friends.

Prayer 213

2 Chronicles 26

Heavenly Father, I hope that I will be successful when I grow up. But I don't want to become like Uzziah. He grew so powerful that he thought he could do anything he wanted. He went into the sanctuary where only priests were allowed to go. No matter what happens, I pray that I will always be humble before You, Lord.

Prayer 214

2 Kings 13

Dear Lord, when Elisha was dying, the king came to him for help because he knew the Syrians were going to attack Israel again. Elisha told the king to shoot an arrow out the window to show that he wanted to save his people from their attackers. Then Elisha told him to hit the ground several times with his arrows. The king did not understand Elisha's directions. He struck the ground only three times. Elisha told him that because he had not hit the ground five or six times, his people would not be able to defeat their attackers. In my school, many kids have trouble following directions. Some of them just don't listen to the teacher. Dear Lord, I pray that You will help me follow the directions You send, so I won't get lost and confused.

Prayer 215

2 Kings 14–15; Amos

Our religious leaders are important to us, Lord. The people in Bethel did not want to hear what the prophet Amos had to say. They had been living without guidance for too long. People like Amos help guide us and explain Your words to us. Please bless the ministers, Sunday school teachers, and all those who do Your work, dear God.

Prayer 216

Hosea

Thank You for Your forgiveness, Heavenly Father. You always take us back when we stray. You encouraged Hosea to find and forgive his wife, Gomer, who had left him. Gomer's lesson shows us that You are faithful to us even when we turn away from You. Please help me to stay close to You, Lord.

Prayer 217

Jonah 1

Jonah disobeyed You, Lord. He didn't want to do what You asked him to do, so he tried to run away. Sometimes I feel like running away from my troubles, dear Lord. I know You are here with me to help with any problems I have. Please help me to face up to things when I'm asked to do them, even when they seem hard at first, dear God, I pray.

Prayer 218

Jonah 1

When Jonah disobeyed You, Lord, You caused a storm at sea. Jonah told the sailors to throw him overboard in order to calm the ocean. We sometimes hear of people who are willing to risk their lives to save others. Bless them for their courage, dear Lord. Please be with our heroes and protect them.

Prayer 219

Jonah 1–4

Dear Lord, Jonah must have been terribly frightened when he was in the big fish's belly. He had to trust You very much to believe he would get out alive. And You were very forgiving to save him because Jonah had not wanted to do what You had asked him at first. Thank You for saving Jonah, dear Lord. I pray that when I feel You are asking me to do something, I won't hesitate.

Prayer 220

2 Kings 17

Dear Lord, the prophets tried to talk to the people of Israel many times, but the people wouldn't listen. They wanted to do things their way. Despite the warnings, they refused to keep faith in You. Without Your help to save them, the Israelites were captured by the Assyrians. I pray that I will listen to You instead of being stubborn, dear Lord.

Prayer 221

2 Kings 17

We have many places to go to for help, dear Lord. Parents and teachers can help us. Our friends and their parents can sometimes help too. If we have an emergency, we can dial 911. King Ahaz was upset that the Assyrians had taken the Israelites out of their land to live in Assyria, but he did not believe in Your power to help them. He did not know where to go for help. No matter where else we look for help, let us come to You first, dear God. We need Your help most of all.

Prayer 222

2 Kings 16; Isaiah 7

You help us because You love us, Heavenly Father. King Ahaz had the chance to protect his land. But he refused to believe that You would help him, so he had to pay the

Assyrians to protect him. If I really care about someone, I look out for him because I love him, not for what I can get from him. We don't have to "pay" for Your guidance and protection. If we have faith and trust in You, Your help will come. I pray that I will never question that You are looking out for me, dear Lord.

Prayer 223

2 Kings 18–19

Dear Lord, sometimes we really need help, but we're afraid to ask for it. We think we ought to be able to work things out for ourselves. Hezekiah, King Ahaz's son, could not continue to pay the Assyrians as his father had done. When the Assyrians tried to take over, Hezekiah prayed for Your protection. You don't want us to be alone, dear Lord. You'll help us if we ask.

Prayer 224

2 Kings 20

You hear our prayers, dear God. King Hezekiah believed in You and asked You to spare his life. You sent him a sign that You would save him. Signs of Your presence are all around us! We don't have to be afraid, because You are with us. I pray that I never forget that, O Lord.

Prayer 225

2 Kings 21–22

Maybe one reason people don't obey Your rules is because they don't know what they are, Lord. King Josiah had to remind his people about Your rules. Too much time had passed since You had given Your laws to the people, and people had forgotten them. I pray that Your word will be taught around the world so everyone can live better lives. And I pray that I don't forget to reach for my Bible when I want to learn about Your rules, O Lord. The Bible is a great place to start when I need to know what You want me to do.

Prayer 226

2 Kings 22–23

King Josiah tried to bring his people back to You, dear God. He reminded them that You are the one true God. Many people in the Bible thought they could pray to idols. But most idols are made of metal and stone. They can't hear anything! We are Your children, Lord. We know You will listen to us. I hope that when I pray to You, I speak respectfully as You deserve and that I always worship You as the one true God.

Prayer 227

Jeremiah 1

Once again You picked a young person to spread Your word, Lord. Jeremiah needed to tell everyone what would happen to them if they didn't stop worshiping false gods. Children aren't always taken as seriously as adults are, so Jeremiah's job was especially difficult. We know we are important in Your eyes. Heavenly Father, please help us with the tough stuff.

Prayer 228
Jeremiah 27

Dear Lord, You told King Zedekiah to save his kingdom by giving it to the Babylonian king. King Nebuchadnezzar was a better servant to You. But Zedekiah wanted to fight the Babylonians instead. He was afraid of them, and they were from another place. If a person is from a different country or is a different color than we are, we might be afraid to play with her. She might also be afraid to play with us because we are different. I pray that I will treat all people the same, no matter what color of skin they have, what language they speak, or what disability they might have. You made us all, dear Father; we are all loved equally.

Prayer 229

Jeremiah 37–38

Jeremiah didn't give up on You, Lord. He knew his people were in big trouble, and he tried to warn them. Instead of listening to him, they tried to hurt him. If only the rest of the people had been true like Jeremiah, then they could have been saved too. Please help us to be true to You, Lord.

Prayer 230

2 Kings 25

Dear Lord, after Jerusalem was destroyed, the people were very sad. Jeremiah wondered why the people didn't listen to You, Lord. But he stayed with them to help them understand Your word. I pray that the people of the world will open up their ears and hear You, dear God.

Prayer 231

Ezekiel 1–5

Heavenly Father, You sent Ezekiel to teach the prisoners in Babylon about how they had upset You. Not everyone understood that You had allowed Jerusalem to be destroyed because Your people would not follow Your rules. You told Ezekiel to act out Your messages to make sure everyone would be able to understand. Even today, people who can't read can know Your love. I pray that someone new will come to know You today.

Prayer 232

Ezekiel 37

Dear Lord, You showed Ezekiel that You would take Your people back someday. If friends are fighting or families are living apart, You give us hope that things can be okay again. Sometimes the only hope we have is You, dear Lord. Please show us how to live in peace with one another.

Prayer 233

Daniel 1

Dear Lord, people today want the best houses or the finest cars. But what the world calls the "best" is not always what You call the best, Heavenly Father. Daniel and his friends were told they could live like kings and learn how things were done in Babylon. But they wanted to follow Your ways. They knew they did not need to live like kings. You look for the purest hearts and the kindest souls. Dear Lord, I pray that next time I ask my mother for more videos or action figures, I remember the story of Daniel and how humble he was.

Prayer 234

Daniel 2

We ask You for many things, dear Lord. When You answer us, sometimes we get so excited we forget to thank You. Daniel asked You to let him know what King

Nebuchadnezzar's dream was about. He thanked You right away when You answered his prayer. Please accept my thanks, dear God, for all the many wonderful things You have done for me.

Prayer 235

Daniel 2

Dear Lord, people with too much power can forget they are human. They begin to think of themselves as gods. Daniel knew the meaning of dreams. He told King Nebuchadnezzar that his dream meant that he was a very powerful ruler. But the dream also showed that Nebuchadnezzar was much less powerful than You, Lord. You teach us that all people have "feet of clay." We can all stumble or be knocked down because we are all human. I pray that I won't forget to keep my own feet firmly on the ground! I am just a regular person, after all.

Prayer 236

Daniel 3

Dear Lord, when King Nebuchadnezzar built a great statue of himself and told everyone to bow down before it, Shadrach, Meshach, and Abednego made a choice to obey You instead of their king, dear Father. They knew they would be punished, but they couldn't turn away from You, Lord. Help me to make the right decisions even though they may not always be the most popular ones, dear Lord.

Prayer 237

Daniel 3

Heavenly Father, King Nebuchadnezzar threw Shadrach, Meshach, and Abednego into a furnace to punish them for disobeying him. He made the fire so hot that his own men got burned. That's what can happen when people are mean to others—their meanness backfires and hurts them instead. Thank You for protecting us, Lord.

Prayer 238

Daniel 3

Thank You, Lord, for saving Shadrach, Meshach, and Abednego. They walked out of the furnace without a scratch! Once King Nebuchadnezzar saw Your power, he wanted to follow You. He saw how You take care of those who are faithful to You. Lord, I pray that I don't have to see a miracle to believe in You.

Prayer 239

Daniel 4

We call to You quickly when we're in trouble, dear Father. Then, when things start going better, we get busy and forget to say our prayers. King Nebuchadnezzar was very proud of his grand kingdom, but he forgot to thank You for all that You'd done to make it so strong. If we don't have a problem to pray about, that's the time to praise You, dear Lord!

Prayer 240

Daniel 4

Dear Lord, King Nebuchadnezzar became boastful about his great kingdom and did not remember to praise You. He took all the credit! It took him seven years of living the life of a beast to remember to honor You as the only true King. I wouldn't want to live my life apart from You, Heavenly Father. That would be like leaving my home and going to live in the desert. I pray that when I brag about something I've done, I remember where it came from, Lord.

Prayer 241

Daniel 5

Dear God, when King Belshazzar used the golden cups that were stolen from Your temple, You sent him a message to let him know that it made You unhappy. Lord, You don't send us notes, but we can still see Your "writing on the wall." If we behave badly over and over again, we will receive our punishment somewhere down the line. If we follow You, You will guide and protect us. Dear Lord, I pray that I don't ignore You when You are trying to tell me something. I hope to keep my eyes open so I can receive Your word.

Prayer 242
Daniel 6

Dear Lord, when Daniel was made ruler of one of the Babylonian regions and an important advisor to the king, many of the other advisors became jealous. They knew that Daniel was Your faithful servant, Lord. So they passed a law saying no one could worship anyone except the king. Anyone who broke the law would be killed. Dear Lord, we are so blessed to live in a place where we are free to worship You. Today in some countries it is against the law to pray! Please help Your followers in these places, Lord.

Prayer 243

Daniel 6

Dear Lord, Daniel continued to pray to You even though he was risking his life. When he was caught, he was thrown into a pit filled with hungry lions! Daniel was not afraid because his faith in You, Lord, was bigger than his fear. Because he was loyal, You would not let the lions hurt him. Thank You for saving Daniel, dear Father.

Prayer 244

Daniel 9, 12

Dear Lord, an angel visited Daniel to tell him many exciting things. A savior was coming, and Daniel must rebuild the city of Jerusalem, the angel said. He must have wondered how that was going to happen, but he trusted You, Heavenly Father. Please help me to be patient and not question Your ways.

Prayer 245

Ezra 1–3

Heavenly Father, just as You promised, the people of Jerusalem got to go home again after many years. They were so happy to be back that they didn't mind all the work they had to do. Please help all those who are away from their homes, dear God. Please bring them home safely.

Prayer 246

Ezra 4–6

Dear Lord, it helps if we have someone older or stronger on our side. When the Israelites returned to Jerusalem to rebuild their temple, many people tried to stop them. But King Cyrus would not let the others bother the Israelites. Sometimes I have to deal with bullies who want to hurt my feelings or steal the ball I'm playing with. I can always turn to an older person for help. I pray that when I get older, I will help out the younger children when they are in trouble.

Prayer 247

Nehemiah 1–4

Dear Lord, most times we don't ask for trouble—it just comes along. Nehemiah worried about his people in Jerusalem, so he returned to help them. He and his workers had to ignore the troublemakers who tried to get them to leave. If another child starts saying mean things and tries to start a fight with me, it's better to ignore him and walk away. Please help me to stay out of trouble's path, dear Lord. But if someone comes along who seems to be a troublemaker, let me trust my instincts and go my own way.

Prayer 248

Esther 1

Dear Lord, people who hurt others often make themselves unhappy too. King Ahasuerus, ruler of the Persian Empire, sent his wife away for disobeying him.

But he soon grew lonely for her company. He had treated her badly and then felt sorry about it. The way we treat others always comes back to us. Help us to treat each other kindly, dear God.

Prayer 249

Esther 2–3

No one can force people to be respectful, Lord. A leader in the Persian palace named Haman commanded everyone to bow down before him, but Mordecai, who worked in the palace, refused. He would only worship You. Making people do things that are against what they believe only makes them angry. Many leaders in the past didn't understand that. I pray that our leaders will be wiser.

Prayer 250

Esther 3

Dear God, because Mordecai would not bow down before him, Haman got very angry. He did not like that the Jews followed Your laws above all others. Haman decided to convince the king to allow all the Jews to be killed. In our world, not everyone believes the way we do, dear Lord. We might think that what they believe is wrong. Still, they are people just like us. With Your help, Lord, we will find a way to live in peace.

Prayer 251

Esther 4–5

Heavenly Father, courageous people feel fear—but unlike cowardly people they find it in themselves to go ahead with their plans even though they feel scared. Queen Esther knew she had to try to help her people, but she was afraid to ask the king to hear her. Because so many lives were at stake, she knew she had to do it anyway. A lot of our courage comes from You, dear Lord. I pray for the courage to do what's right.

Prayer 252

Esther 5

Dear Lord, humans are not toys to be played with and thrown around. People have souls. Haman thought that Mordecai was a problem he could get rid of easily. He did not see him as a person. Mistreating others is very bad in Your eyes, dear God. If I have a problem with someone, please help me to find a fair solution.

Prayer 253

Esther 6

Dear Lord, Haman thought that having Mordecai killed would solve his problem. He should have left Mordecai alone. Haman's plan backfired because Mordecai had saved the king's life. The king wanted to see him honored, not hanged. Please help me to remember that it's not fair to blame others for our problems, dear Lord.

Prayer 254

Esther 7–8

O Lord, King Ahasuerus realized that Haman's law that all Jews be killed was cruel, but it was too late to change it. Instead, the king signed a new law that allowed the Jews to defend themselves against their attackers. He wanted to give them a fair chance. When two teams play each other, they have to play by the same rules and use the same equipment. That makes the game more fair. I hope that, like Ahasuerus, I give others a fair chance. I know You are a just God, and You would want it that way.

Prayer 255

Job 1

Heavenly Father, it seems that Satan goes around looking for trouble. He believed that Job, Your faithful servant, would not be so loyal to You if all the good things in his life were taken away. Satan wanted to tempt Job to do something wrong. Satan wants to turn us away from You, Lord. Dear God, I pray that if terrible things start happening to me, I won't question my faith in You. Please help me keep my faith strong.

Prayer 256

Job 1–2

Dear Lord, You allowed Satan to try to tempt Job because You knew Job would not give in. It is hard to imagine how anyone could stand up to Satan's test as Job did. Without his strong faith, Job never would have made it. Show me how to make my faith stronger, Heavenly Father.

Prayer 257

Job 2–37

Job knew that he had done nothing wrong in Your eyes, Lord. But he didn't understand why such awful things were happening to him. When someone gets sick or has some trouble, it doesn't mean she has been a bad person. We don't know why one person gets sick and another stays well. That is for You to know, dear God. Please help us to accept the things we can't change and to trust in You, Lord.

Prayer 258

Job 38–42

Dear God, we wonder why bad things have to happen to good people. Job could not understand why You would allow such terrible things to happen to him. You reminded him that You do not need to explain Yourself to anyone. There are many things we do not know, dear Lord. There are some things we will never understand in this world, but that's okay. We trust Your will, Heavenly Father.

Prayer 259

Malachi

You sent us the promise of a Savior, dear Lord—one who would make our hearts pure. The prophet Malachi told Your people that one day they would stand before You and be judged for their faithfulness. The Savior would prepare them for that day. What a fantastic blessing, Lord! Thank You for the best gift You could have ever given us.

Prayer 260

Luke 1

Dear Lord, You rewarded many of Your followers with children. Zacharias and Elizabeth, his wife, wanted very much to have a child, but they thought they were too old. You sent the angel Gabriel to tell them that they would soon have a child and that they should name him John. All through the Bible, children are treated as blessings. We know from reading the Scriptures how important we are to You. Thank You for loving us and for making our dreams come true, when it is part of Your plan.

Prayer 261

Luke 1

Dear Lord, children ask a lot of questions. Even adults think they need to have all the answers. Zacharias doubted what Gabriel told him about the son he would have. He could not see how it would be possible. We want to know how things happen and why. We don't need to question You, Heavenly Father. We only have to trust You. I pray that I won't question the good things in life that happen to me, but instead that I will accept them with gladness.

Prayer 262

Luke 1

Dear God, You picked a special woman named Mary to be the mother of Your Son. She lived in Nazareth and was engaged to marry a carpenter named Joseph. Mary was not a queen. She was just a simple woman who loved You. Thank You, Lord, for choosing Mary.

Prayer 263

Luke 1

Dear God, the baby John had not yet been born when Mary came to visit. Elizabeth was excited because she knew that Mary would give birth to a very special baby. Even baby John knew! Elizabeth felt him leap for joy because he knew that the Savior would be born soon. I feel joy in my heart when I think of You, too, Holy Father.

Prayer 264

Luke 1

Dear Lord, many people knew that the coming of the Savior would be a very important event. Your prophets had been telling people of His coming for hundreds of years. When the baby John was born, his parents knew that when he grew up, he would go across the land to tell the good news of Your Son's birth, dear Lord. You sent John the Baptist to get people ready for Jesus. I pray that I stay ready for Jesus' return by always doing my best and being a good person, O Lord.

Prayer 265

Luke 2

Jesus was born on a bed of hay,
Surrounded by animals
That watched as He lay.

His mother and Joseph
Were close by His side.
While His Father rejoiced
From His kingdom on high.

Sometimes I want to pray to You in poetry, dear God.

Prayer 266

Luke 2

Dear Lord, the night Jesus was born, an angel appeared to shepherds who were spending the night in their fields. The angel told them what had happened and where to find the new baby. As soon as they found Jesus, the shepherds ran to tell everyone they saw about the Savior. Let's do the same thing today. The more people hear about Jesus, the more they can know Your love, dear Father. I pray that You show me the way to spread the news of Your love to other people.

Prayer 267

Matthew 2

Dear Lord, You sent the news of Jesus' birth to shepherds and wise men alike. King Herod also learned about the birth of Jesus and tried to get the wise men to tell him where He was. Herod did not like the idea of a king of the Jews. Jesus was going to have a tough life with bad people like Herod against Him. Even though You knew some people would resist, You sent the Savior so that everyone could know You better. Thank You, Lord, for sending Jesus.

Prayer 268

Matthew 2

The gifts the wise men brought Jesus were very special, Lord. Not only did they bring Jesus gold and special spices, but they decided not to tell Herod where to find the baby. On Christmas and on birthdays, we get gifts too. But no gift is as great as the one You gave us, Heavenly Father. Thank You for sending Jesus to the world to save us from sin.

Prayer 269

Matthew 2

Thank You for sending Your angel to warn Joseph, dear Lord. He moved his family to Egypt to protect Jesus from King Herod. You made sure Jesus was safe until it was time to return to Israel. If You had not kept Jesus safe, think what a different world we would have today! Jesus taught us a lot of important lessons about love and kindness. Thank You, Lord, for sending Your Son.

Prayer 270

Luke 2

Dear Lord, when Jesus was a boy, Mary and Joseph took Him to Jerusalem for the Passover. When they left to return to Nazareth, they realized that Jesus was not with them. Later they found Him in the temple. They hadn't thought to look there at first, but later it made sense that He had gone there to be with You, dear God. Even at that young age, Jesus was drawn to You and Your word, Lord. He was a very special boy who grew to be a very special man. Thank You for sending us Your Son.

Prayer 271

Luke 3

John, the son of Zacharias and Elizabeth, had a big job preparing the people to meet Jesus, Lord. He asked everyone to be sorry for their sins. Then, with the water of the Jordan River, he baptized the people who had listened to him and understood his message. Still, some people wanted to do things their own way instead of obeying Your laws, Father. Lots of people are still like that today. Dear God, I pray that when I sin against You, I will be sorry for my sin and accept Your forgiveness.

Prayer 272

Luke 3

Dear Lord, John baptized people with water as a sign that they were turning away from their sin. He did this for so many people that they began to call him John the Baptist. I pray that You will forgive my sins, Heavenly Father. Bless me and keep my heart pure. I pray in the name of Your Son, Jesus Christ, Amen.

Prayer 273

Matthew 3

Dear God, here is a verse for You.

A dove flew down, the Holy Spirit,
To tell us of the Savior.
"He is my Son," said the Spirit to John.
"To Him I give my favor."

Prayer 274

Matthew 4

Dear Lord, when Jesus went into the desert for forty days and nights, Satan tried to tempt Him to disobey You. That was a long time to be tempted. I know that when a friend asks me to do something I shouldn't (for example, skip my homework to play outside), I feel less and less sure of myself the more he asks me. But Satan was no match for Jesus. He tried everything to get

Jesus to give in, but Jesus outsmarted him every time. I know that if You and Jesus are on my side, Lord, I don't have to be afraid of Satan's power. I pray that whatever temptations come my way, I remember who is on "my team."

Prayer 275

Mark 1

Dear Lord, Jesus called some fishermen to become His followers. I think it was important to Him that they were ordinary men. They weren't priests or religious leaders. As fishermen they had to work hard just to make a living. But Jesus said, "I'll make you fishers of men." Then, they went out to preach Your word, Heavenly Father. They didn't question Jesus when He asked them to stop whatever they were doing. That took a lot of faith on their part. I pray to have faith that strong, Lord, whenever I am called to do Your work.

Prayer 276

John 2

Dear Lord, Jesus and His mother, Mary, went to a wedding in Cana. When the party ran out of wine, Jesus thought it was too soon to test His power. But Mary knew it was time. Timing is important. If we rush through a task or don't finish our work, it can be as bad as if we didn't do it at all. But if we never take action, no one will know what we can do. Your timing is perfect, dear Lord. Help me to know when the time is right to act.

Prayer 277

John 2

News spread quickly after Jesus did His first miracle, Lord. He had turned the water to wine and allowed the wedding celebration to continue. Jesus did many other things too, like being kind to strangers and giving food to the hungry. I can't make miracles happen, but I can do some of the other things Jesus did. Lord, please help me to be like Jesus every day.

Prayer 278

Mark 1

Dear Lord, Jesus performed miracles by healing the sick. Today, doctors and other healers help sick people, but they don't cure with miracles like Jesus did. With Your help though, dear Lord, doctors can help even very sick people to get better. I pray for all people who need Your healing touch, dear God.

Prayer 279

Mark 2

Dear Lord, folks came from miles around to see Jesus. They all believed that He could help them, and He did! I wasn't alive back then to see Jesus. Still, I feel Him in my heart whenever I pray. Thank You for being with me, Jesus.

Prayer 280

Mark 2

Dear God, Jesus came to save the sinners who needed to hear His message of forgiveness. Some of His followers did not like it when He spent time with these people. They did not realize that Jesus spent time with people who might be called a "bad crowd" today because He knew they needed His help most of all. They needed Him and He was there for them. Lord, please help me to see the good in people who sometimes do bad things.

Prayer 281

Mark 3

Dear God, some people would say that Jesus had a lot of common sense. He knew that it was wrong to work on the Sabbath. But He also knew that it was wrong to let someone suffer and not do anything about it. Healing a sick man on the Sabbath made Jesus unpopular with many religious leaders. Jesus knew He had made the right choice. Help us to decide what is most important and what is Your will, dear Lord.

Prayer 282

John 3

Dear Lord, the religious leaders who did not like what Jesus was doing thought they had all the answers. But they did not know You the way Jesus did. Jesus told a man named Nicodemus that a body is born only once but that the spirit must be born again. This confused Nicodemus. I know that Jesus meant that to be "born again" we should allow the Holy Spirit to guide us to believe in Jesus as our Lord and Savior. I pray that the Holy Spirit will come into my life and help me to be "born again."

Prayer 283

John 3

Thank You for Your love, Heavenly Father. Thank You for sending Your Son to take away our sins. Jesus compared Himself to a light shining on the earth. Some people tried to hide from the light so their bad deeds wouldn't be seen. But others loved the light and wanted You to see their goodness. I pray that Your light will shine on us so we won't live in darkness anymore.

Prayer 284

John 4

Dear Lord, the Samaritan woman Jesus met at the well had made many mistakes. Some people thought she wasn't good enough for Jesus to spend time with. Jesus forgave the woman for all her sins so she could be pure again. Bless You, Jesus, for

You know that all people do the wrong thing sometimes. Because of You, I can know forgiveness.

Prayer 285

John 4

Dear Lord, the nobleman in Cana knew how powerful Jesus was—not because he had seen the great things Jesus was capable of doing but because he had faith in Him. Jesus knew this and healed the man's sick son without even needing to see him! I read about "miracle cures" and watch "miracle rescues" on television. If we have true faith, we don't need to be surrounded by miracles and signs to believe in You, Lord. Faith means believing in things we can't always see and feel. Dear Lord, I pray that my faith stays strong through all things.

Prayer 286

Mark 6

Dear Lord, bad things can happen when people get more power than they can handle. When John the Baptist criticized King Herod's marriage to his brother's wife, Herodias, she became angry and asked that John be killed. Even though he knew John was a good man, Herod did what Herodias asked. He didn't want to be seen as a weak ruler. Lord, Your power is great and wise. I pray I will always trust Your power over the power of men.

Prayer 287

Matthew 5; Luke 6

Dear God, when Jesus taught from the mountain, He reminded His followers that they must behave kindly toward others, and they must also think well of them. Father, help me to behave kindly toward others as

Jesus taught us to do. Help me to be careful about the things I think and do. I pray that I will fill my mind and heart with good things so I will stay pure.

Prayer 288

Matthew 7

Dear God, Jesus told stories with lessons, called parables, to give His followers examples of how they should live their lives. One story was about two different houses. The first house was built on a rock. The other house was built on sand. The house that was built well stood up against all kinds of weather. The other house was swept away with the first heavy rain. Help me to build a strong foundation in my life, Lord. Teach me to make good plans and to think things through before I act. Teach me also to be careful in the ways I treat people. Each day I pray that I will follow Your Golden Rule, dear Lord: Do unto others the way you would have others do unto you.

Prayer 289

Mark 4

Dear God, Jesus told a story about seeds. Growing plants takes a lot of work. First, there must be good soil to plant the seeds in. By bad soil, I think Jesus meant that some people listen to You, God, and follow Your ways for a time, but then they don't have what it takes to keep following You. But, if we spread Your word, we will be like a good gardener that "feeds and waters" the soil to support others in their faith. If a gardener takes care of the plant, it will bear flowers and fruit. It will be worth all the hard work. I pray that I learn to look at Your words as seeds, Lord, so I can help Your message take root in others and grow to be strong.

Prayer 290

Matthew 13

Dear God, Jesus' stories about the yeast that makes dough rise and the tiny mustard seeds that grow into big plants made me think that even small things can be very powerful. With something like faith, a little goes a long way. Dear God, I pray that my faith will help me to bloom like a beautiful flower. I pray that the faith in me will rise like dough and spread around to everyone I meet.

Prayer 291

Mark 4

Dear God, Jesus' friends got very worried when the storm came up and threatened to sink their boat. Jesus told the wind and the rain to be still. As quickly as that, the storm was over! His friends had forgotten how powerful You are. Sometimes I get scared when bad storms come. The lightning and thunder make me afraid. Dear Father, You have the power to quiet the winds. I pray that You will keep me safe until the storms pass by.

Prayer 292

Mark 5

Dear God, the man who had been attacked by evil spirits recognized Jesus coming toward him. The demons grew very afraid and were forced to leave the man's body. Demons run away when they see You, Lord. You are stronger than all the evil in the world. I pray that if I am ever pursued by my own demons, my faith in You will chase them away too.

Prayer 293

Mark 5

Dear God, the people who had faith in Jesus were cured of their sickness. Jesus visited lots of places, so many people could see Him and be healed. A woman in one crowd was healed just by touching His sleeve, simply because she had faith in Him. Thank You, Jesus, for helping so many people.

Prayer 294

Mark 5

Dear God, Jairus's neighbors told him his little girl was dead. Jesus said, "She is only sleeping." Then, He brought her back to life. Many people believe only what they can see. You tell us to believe what we can't see, dear Lord. Help me to believe in Your power, God, even when others doubt it.

Prayer 295

Matthew 9

Dear Lord, the Pharisees heard about the work Jesus was doing, and it made them nervous. They did not like the fact that Jesus was becoming so popular. When the Pharisees heard the story about Jesus ordering the demons to leave the sick man's body, they wanted to believe that only an evil person could talk to demons. They did not understand that Your goodness is more powerful than anything, dear Father. The next time I see a movie or a television show with a scary, powerful villain, let me remember who has the real power in the world—those who fight for good!

Prayer 296

Luke 7

Dear Lord, some people wondered why Jesus spent so much time with outcasts. Many people thought that if He was truly Your Son, those people weren't worth His time. Even though the Jewish leaders did not like it, Jesus often forgave people who had committed many, many sins. Some people make little mistakes, and some make big ones. If the people who make big mistakes are truly sorry, You will forgive them too, Heavenly Father. You want all people to be by Your side. Thank You, Lord, for being so loving.

Prayer 297

Luke 7

Dear Lord, when Jesus was walking through the town of Nain one day, He and His followers saw a funeral procession. The person who had died was a young man much loved by his mother. The young man's mother was very sad because she had recently lost her husband too. You knew she had faith, so You helped to take away her pain by bringing her son back to life. We are so thankful for Your kindness. When we read about You, we begin to learn how we should treat each other. I pray that I will learn from Jesus' example and help others who are in pain too.

Prayer 298

Luke 9

Dear God, Jesus had spent a lot of time with the disciples. He taught them everything they needed to know about spreading

Your word. The disciples went out into the land with only the clothes on their backs to tell the people the good news about Jesus. Your message is simple, dear Lord. All people have to do is listen. I pray that I am always open to Your wishes and that I listen to You, my parents, and my friends when they are trying to tell me something they think is important.

Prayer 299

Mark 6

Dear God, crowds began to follow Jesus wherever He went. One day a hungry crowd of five thousand people gathered to hear Jesus speak. The disciples knew that there was not enough food to feed the whole crowd. But Jesus blessed the small amount of fish and bread and managed to feed everyone! You provide for our needs in many ways. Thank You, Heavenly Father.

Prayer 300

Mark 6; Matthew 14

Dear God, the disciples loved Jesus and believed in Him, but they still had trouble believing some of the miracles they saw. Peter saw Jesus walking across the water to the boat. When Peter tried to walk out to meet Jesus, he walked several steps but then he began to sink! Peter became scared and forgot to have faith. The disciples were like us because we only know the ways of the world. The ways of Your kingdom are so much more wonderful, dear Lord!

Prayer 301

Matthew 15

Your help is there for anyone who asks for it, dear God. While Jesus was traveling with His friends, a Canaanite woman came to Him and asked if He would cure her sick daughter. Although the woman was not an Israelite, Jesus healed her daughter because

He saw how much faith the woman had in Him. You are never too busy to make time for anyone who believes. Thank You, Lord, for listening to us all.

Prayer 302

Mark 7

Dear God, Jesus didn't do His miracles to get attention for Himself. He only wanted to help others and show them Your love. When news got out about how Jesus could heal people—such as the deaf man who lived by the Sea of Galilee—everyone wanted to turn Him into a celebrity. They wanted to make Him famous! Jesus only wanted them to love You and to be thankful to You. Please help us all to be unselfish, Lord.

Prayer 303

Mark 8

Dear God, many people followed Jesus just to see and hear Him for themselves. Jesus wanted to take care of the large crowds that gathered to listen to Him. More than once, Jesus provided food for everyone from just a few loaves of bread and a couple of fish. Everyone got to experience Jesus' love for them! The people whom Jesus helped were so overjoyed that they couldn't stop themselves from telling everyone what Jesus had done. When Jesus healed a blind man, He told the man not to stop and tell people what had happened. Today, we don't need to hide our joy from the world. I pray for the courage to tell everyone about the great things You have done for us, Lord!

Prayer 304

Mark 8

Even though each person Jesus helped wanted to tell everyone else all about Him, Jesus wanted to hide who He was from His enemies. He had a lot of work to do to spread Your word, dear God. His enemies wanted to stop Him from doing His job. Jesus told His disciples that many amazing things would happen to Him, but He had so much to do first! All this was part of Your perfect plan, Lord. Please help me to understand the plans You had for Jesus and why He had to go through what He did. And please help me to know that even though everything that happens doesn't make sense at the time, it is happening for a reason.

Prayer 305

Mark 8

Dear God, Jesus wanted the people to follow His example of a good life. He told them not to be ashamed to listen to His teachings—even if others wanted to keep doing things their own way. He said that those who refused to follow Him would be turned away at the gates of heaven. If other children make fun of me for loving You, dear God, help me to stand by You. I don't want You to be ashamed of me. I want to follow You all through my life.

Prayer 306

Mark 9

Dear God, James, John, and Peter could hardly believe their eyes when they saw Moses and Elijah appear beside Jesus on the mountaintop! The two men had been dead for many years. The disciples heard Your voice speaking to them, Lord. You told them to listen to what Jesus had to say because He was Your Son. Jesus later told the disciples not to tell anyone what they had seen until it was time for Him to rise from the dead. James, John, and Peter knew

there was much they didn't understand.
They knew that Jesus was a good teacher
and He would tell them what they needed
to know. I pray that we will learn from Jesus
as the disciples did.

Prayer 307

Mark 9

Dear God, a man with a sick child doubted
that Jesus' disciples could heal people the
way Jesus did. The disciples tried to help
the man's son. Sadly, the man did not
believe in their power as Jesus' friends, so
they could not cure the boy. The man did
not understand that unless he had true faith,
no miracles could happen. Help us to have
faith in all Your servants, dear Lord.

Prayer 308

Mark 9

Dear Lord, my friends and I sometimes
argue about which one of us is better at one

thing or another. We all want to be the best sometimes. That makes us a little bit selfish. The disciples were not perfect either. They wanted to know who Jesus thought was the best disciple among them. Jesus told them that the one who put himself last behind the others would be first to Him. Lord, help me try to be the best I can be. Help me learn to serve others before myself. Being number one isn't the only thing to strive for.

Prayer 309

Matthew 20

Dear God, it's hard for me to understand how, in Your eyes, finishing last could be the same as finishing first. Jesus compared the kingdom of heaven to a man who hired people to work on his farm. The farmer and his workers agreed on the price he would pay them. Later, some of the workers got upset because they weren't paid extra for working longer days than the others. The rewards in heaven will be the same for everyone, no matter whether people love You their whole lives or come to know You later in life. You love all who do Your work and keep Your laws. Your kingdom is fair. It is not like this world, dear God. I pray that someday I will understand its greatness.

Prayer 310

Luke 10

Dear Lord, I usually think of a neighbor as someone who lives near me. But Jesus taught that a neighbor is anyone who helps another person when needed. The good Samaritan from Jesus' story was the only person who stopped to help the wounded man on the side of the road. Others just passed by. Many people can't see when people are hurting, or they try to ignore it. Sometimes they are afraid to get involved. Bless our neighbors, Lord, and help me to be a good neighbor to them!

Prayer 311

Luke 11

We all know this prayer, dear God, but not all of us know where it came from. When Jesus' disciples asked Him how to pray, He taught this to them:

Our Father who is in heaven,
Holy is Your name.
Your kingdom come, Your will be done,
On Earth as it is in Heaven.
Please give us each day our daily bread,
And forgive our sins, as we forgive those
   who hurt us.
Lead us away from temptation,
And keep us from evil.
For Yours is the kingdom, the power,
   and the glory,
Forever and ever.
Amen.

Prayer 312

Luke 11

Dear Lord, I know You are listening to my prayers. Jesus tells us it is okay to ask You for what we need. Even if You decide not to answer our prayers right away, we can keep asking and expect to get an answer someday. Jesus said that if we keep "knocking at Your door," one day You will open it to us. I will pray to You every day, Lord.

Prayer 313

Luke 12

Dear Lord, my friends and I love to go to the store, even if we can't always get the things we want. It would be nice to have them, but I know that I do not need all that extra stuff. Jesus told His friends that they didn't need to worry about what they would eat or wear. You will give us all that we need. I thank You for the clothes and books and toys that I do have, Lord, but especially for the things that matter—my family and friends.

Prayer 314

Mark 10

Dear God, Jesus met a rich man who asked Him, "What should I do to make sure that I will get to heaven?" Jesus told him that he must give away all his money. Jesus knew that the man did not need all that money to be happy. He also knew that having lots of things tends to make a person selfish—even if he doesn't mean to be. I like my toys and books. It's fun to collect things. Sometimes I get so busy with my toys that I forget to help my mom or play with the baby. I wonder if Jesus would say that things are becoming too important to me. Help me to know what's really important in my life, dear God.

Prayer 315

Mark 10, 12

A person doesn't have to have much to serve You, dear Lord. The rich people in the temple donated handfuls of money, but one little old lady only had two coins to give. Jesus told His disciples that her gift was greater because she gave all that she had. The others gave only a small portion of what they could afford. If I put my allowance into the collection plate at church, it means just as much to You as a rich person putting in a hundred-dollar bill. I pray that I will find joy in giving because You give so much to me every day, Lord.

Prayer 316

Luke 13

Dear Lord, watch over me as the gardener looked after the fig tree in the Bible. The man who owned the tree grew impatient waiting for it to bear fruit, but the gardener asked him to give it more time. The gardener promised that he would give the fig tree special care to help it bloom. Jesus was like that gardener with His people. Just as the gardener wanted a second chance to help the tree grow fruit, Jesus came to earth to give us a second chance to please You. I pray that under Jesus' and Your special care, I can grow to be a good person.

Prayer 317

Luke 14

Dear God, thank You for giving everybody a chance to join You in Your kingdom. In the story that Jesus told the Pharisees, the man who threw the party for his friends became angry when they all said that they had more important things to do. The man decided to invite other people—ones who would appreciate his invitation. Like the man in the story, You will welcome us all to Your house, Lord. We just have to accept

Your invitation. Dear Lord, I pray for my family and friends. I pray that we will all trust Jesus as our Lord and Savior.

Prayer 318

Luke 13

Helping others is our "full-time job." The religious leaders in the temple were upset when Jesus helped the sick woman on the Sabbath. But Jesus reminded them that we don't get days off from helping people. Whether I'm at school, at home, or at church, please show me ways to help others, dear Lord, I pray.

Prayer 319

John 9

Jesus healed the blind beggar so everyone would see how great Your power is, Lord. The disciples thought the man had been punished because of his blindness, but Jesus told them that the man had done nothing wrong. He had been born blind so he could become an example of Your power and love. You blessed him—and us—by making him see again! Thank You, Lord, for Your great power and love.

Prayer 320

John 9

Dear God, the Pharisees tried to figure out who Jesus was. They came up with all kinds of answers, but none of their explanations was right. They even considered Jesus to be a sinner because they could not understand how You could allow Him to work on the Sabbath. The Pharisees were not as faithful as the beggar. They didn't want to accept Jesus as Your Son. The beggar didn't ask any questions, dear Lord—he just believed. I pray that my faith will stay as strong and that I won't question You.

Prayer 321

John 10

Dear God, we will count on You to lead us and care for us like a shepherd cares for his sheep. Sheep know the difference between their shepherd and a thief, Jesus explained. They know who to trust. Jesus knew that good people would know Him for who He was and follow Him without asking lots of questions. I pray that my faith allows no doubt, Lord.

Prayer 322

Luke 15

Dear Lord, I pray for the people who are like lost lambs. When the religious leaders became angry with Jesus for spending time with sinners, He told them that You are happiest when the people You think You have lost come back to You. I pray that You will find the lost members of Your flock and bring them home to You.

Prayer 323

Luke 15

Heavenly Father, You look after all of Your children. When one is lost, You will be sad until that one is found. Jesus helped His people understand this by telling a story about a woman who had ten coins and then lost one. The other nine were important, but the tenth was just as valuable to her. Because it had been lost, she was especially happy when she found it. Sometimes I feel confused, and I question why bad things have to happen. When I feel this way, I feel like I am walking alone in a dark forest. If I am ever lost, not just in body but in spirit too, I pray You will look for me until You find me, Lord.

Prayer 324

Luke 15

Dear Lord, sometimes I complain that there are too many rules. Just like the runaway son in Jesus' story, I sometimes think it would be cool to make up my own rules. But then I stop and remember that none of us is free if we don't have You to guide us, dear Lord. The son in the story didn't realize this right away. He went out and lived by his own rules and wasted all the money his father had given him. Please help me, Lord, to be respectful of my parents and to always keep Your rules. Otherwise, just like the prodigal son, I will be lost without You.

Prayer 325

Luke 15

Dear God, in Jesus' story, the runaway son came home to his father. He ran out of money and realized that he wasn't happy living a life where he could do whatever he wanted. The father was very happy to welcome his son back, but the brother who had stayed home became jealous. He was mad that their father could forgive his brother so easily. He wanted his father to love him more because he had had to work very hard to help him. Dear Lord, like the father in the story, You have enough love to share with all Your children!

Prayer 326

Luke 16

Dear God, Jesus knew that money was very important to some people. But I know from Jesus' story that unless we share what we have with others, money is really no good to us. It doesn't make us better people, Lord, and it can't buy Your forgiveness. The rich man didn't understand this. He thought he had everything he needed. He didn't help the beggar living right outside his house. In the end, the rich man wound up with nothing. The beggar had nothing while he lived on the earth. When he got to heaven, You took care of him, dear God.

Prayer 327

Matthew 18

We ask Your forgivness, dear God, but sometimes we forget that it's just as important to forgive each other. In another of Jesus' stories, the king canceled a debt one of his servants owed him. Then the servant went out and demanded that another person repay him the money he was owed. The king became angry because his servant had not shown the same generosity. In my life I expect to be forgiven for the thoughtless things I do, but I pray that I also remember to forgive other people when they are sorry.

Prayer 328

Mark 10

Dear Lord, sometimes I think the things I say and do don't matter because I'm just a child. But Jesus loved children for being so trusting and innocent. The disciples thought the boys and girls were getting in Your way. But Jesus took them in His arms and told the crowd how important little children are to You! Thank You, Jesus, for blessing the children.

Prayer 329

Luke 17

Dear God, Jesus told ten men how they could be cured of their illness. It worked— they were healed! The men went on their way. Only one man stopped to thank Jesus. Saying thank-you is very important. If I forget to say it, my mom reminds me. Dear Father, I pray that I don't forget to thank You every day for all You've done for me, my family, and my friends. Amen.

Prayer 330

John 11

Dear Lord, we don't understand why You allow some things to happen. We can't see what Your purpose is. That's why we need faith. In our hearts we know everything happens for the best. Mary and Martha, Jesus' friends, were very upset when their brother, Lazarus, became sick. Jesus cared very much for Lazarus. He knew he could make Lazarus live again. Lord, help me believe in Your plans for us when everything looks bleak.

Prayer 331

John 11

Dear Lord, Lazarus's sister Mary believed in Jesus so much that she believed that Lazarus could live again after he had died. Mary knew that no one but Your Son could make that happen, Lord! But the wonderful thing is, You gave us Jesus to be "the resurrection" for us all. That means that if we believe in Him, we will live forever. Thank You, Lord, for giving us life after death.

Prayer 332

John 11

Jesus knew how sad Mary and her friends felt. He cried with them because He cared so much. Then he prayed to You, Heavenly Father, and Lazarus came back to life! Others had been brought back to life by the prophets Elijah and Elisha. But Lazarus had been buried already! When Lazarus came out of the tomb, many people were afraid. Sometimes people fear what they don't understand. Please help me to see Your miracles as acts of love, dear God.

Prayer 333

John 12

Dear God, Jesus was thankful to Mary for the perfume she poured on His head. Perfume was very expensive then, and Mary had been saving it for a long time. Judas criticized her for not selling the perfume for money to use for the poor, but Jesus knew that Mary didn't have much to give. He was grateful that she had saved her best gift for Him. Please help us to learn from Mary and give our best to You, dear Lord.

Prayer 334

Mark 10

Bartimaeus, a blind man, tried to get Jesus' attention while Jesus was telling His stories. Jesus heard him even though the crowd was very loud. Even though Bartimaeus couldn't see, he knew Jesus could help him. He called Jesus "Lord," so Jesus knew he had faith. I pray that You will hear me above the crowd too, dear Lord. I pray that my faith will guide me even when there are things I can't see or understand.

Prayer 335

Luke 19

Dear God, Zacchaeus, like Bartimaeus, tried hard to see Jesus. He was short, so to see above the crowd he had to climb a tree. Jesus must have known that someone who tried so hard to see Him must believe in Him. Jesus stayed at Zacchaeus's house, even though Zacchaeus was a tax collector. People criticized Jesus because they did not like tax collectors. But the next day, Zacchaeus was a changed man! He said he would give half of everything he owned to the poor. Just as Jesus loved the poor, He loved the rich who humbled themselves before Him. Lord, help me to see that it's not the size of someone's wallet that counts, but what is in his heart.

Prayer 336

Luke 19

Jesus chose a little donkey for His ride to Jerusalem, dear God. This king didn't need a grand horse to show His power. Jesus had Your power! I pray that I can be as humble, Lord, and remember all the wonderful things Jesus taught us.

Prayer 337

Luke 19

Dear Lord, some days all I want is to have lots of friends. Then I would be happy. When Jesus went into Jerusalem, people lined the streets to see Him. The crowds cheered and put palm fronds in His path. But Jesus cried for the ones who weren't there. He wanted everyone to be saved from their sins. Jesus cared more about the fate of each individual than whether He had lots of fans. I pray that I value each and every one of my friends, and not just how big a group I hang out with. And I hope everyone can be saved one day so Jesus won't be sad any more.

Prayer 338

Luke 19

The temple was a special place to worship You, dear God. Jesus got angry when He saw that the people were using it as a place to buy and sell things. He didn't think they were being respectful. I hope I will have the opportunity to volunteer and clean up our church building, so I can show how much it means to me. Please help us to keep our churches holy, dear God.

Prayer 339

Luke 20

The Pharisees didn't want to believe Jesus, and they were jealous of His popularity. They even tried to explain away Jesus' miracles. They didn't want to give up their money and power. Please help us not to be like the Pharisees, dear Lord. When we see something that seems amazing, help us to know that all incredible things come from You.

Prayer 340

Mark 12

When we follow You, Lord, it doesn't mean we forget all about this world. If we owe someone money, we should pay him. This might have been what Jesus meant when He said, "Give Caesar what is owed to Caesar, and give God what is owed to God." We give You our love and faith, dear God— things that money can't buy. But it costs money to run our government, so we must pay our taxes. Living for You means doing the right thing. I pray that I will learn to give gladly, and not try to hold on to all the money and things I have for myself.

Prayer 341

Matthew 25

Dear God, no one knows when Jesus will come back. When Jesus was alive, He wanted to prepare the people for His death and resurrection. But He wanted them to know that they should always be ready for His return. He told a story about some women who took their lamps and went to meet a bridegroom. Five of them didn't bring extra oil, and five did. The lamps of those who didn't bring extra oil burned out. The women missed the bridegroom and the wedding feast because they were stuck in the dark. I think that our good deeds and the way we care about each other are like the oil for the lamps. Jesus wants us to obey You and love one another, so we will always be prepared for when He returns. I pray that whenever that time comes, I will be ready to meet Him!

Prayer 342

Matthew 25

If we do something for others, Jesus told His disciples, it is like doing something for Him. When I rake the leaves for the older lady down the street or give gloves to a homeless person in the winter, I am doing these things for Jesus too. Please help me to do something good for Jesus every day, Heavenly Father!

Prayer 343

Matthew 26

Dear Lord, I am as greedy as the next person. When I go into a toy store, I see so many things I want. When I don't have money to pay for them, it's very frustrating. But Judas, one of Jesus' disciples, was willing to betray his friend and Lord for money. That was terrible! Money can buy a lot of things, but it can't buy the most important thing. When we share Your love with others, we are the richest people in the world, dear Father!

Prayer 344

Matthew 26; Luke 22

Dear Lord, the man whose house Jesus used for the Passover Feast was ready for Him. He had the table set and the food prepared. Will we be ready when Jesus calls for us? I pray that we will, Lord.

Prayer 345

Matthew 26

Dear God, at the Last Supper Jesus broke bread and gave it to His disciples. He told them it was His body, and He wanted them to eat it and remember Him. Then He took wine and passed it around. "This is My blood," He said. "Drink it and remember Me." He was giving His disciples and us a way to remember just how much He loves us—for He knew He would soon suffer and give His life for us. When I take communion, I pray that I will remember Jesus and all He has done for the world. Thank You, Lord, for the greatest gift of all, Your Son Jesus.

Prayer 346

John 13

Dear Lord, please help us to treat each other the way Jesus treated His disciples. When He started to wash their feet with water, Peter objected. He thought that Jesus should act like a master, and they should act like His servants. But Jesus said that He wanted them to do this kind of thing for one another. Jesus knew it was important to treat others as equals. Everyone is worthy of love before the Lord. No one is better than anyone else. Help us to be kind and fair to each other, Lord.

Prayer 347

John 13

Dear God, Peter wanted to know who would be the one to betray Jesus. He never dreamed that he would be the one who would pretend not to know Jesus. We don't always know what's in our hearts, Lord, but You do. I pray that when my friends at school make fun of my faith or use Jesus' name in vain, I won't betray Jesus myself by refusing to speak up or by taking part in it. Please give me the strength to be true to my faith, Lord.

Prayer 348

Mark 14

When Jesus was in the garden praying, He wondered if there was any way You could spare him, Lord. Still, He was willing to accept Your perfect plan, even though it meant He would suffer. It's too bad His disciples couldn't have stayed awake to pray with Him in His hour of need. It's easy to be a friend when everything is going right. Sometimes when my friends are sad, I don't know what to say to them or how to help them. I hope I can just listen and be there for them, though. Please help me to be a good friend in good times and bad, Lord.

Prayer 349

John 18

Dear God, Jesus knew Judas would betray Him, but He didn't run away or confront Judas. Jesus also knew that He might have been able to escape the soldiers who came for Him when Peter pulled out his sword. But Jesus told Peter to put away his sword because it was God's plan. Jesus was ready for whatever lay ahead. Please help me to understand and accept the things in life I can't change, Lord, even suffering and death. It helps to put myself in Your hands.

Prayer 350

Matthew 26; Mark 14

The priests didn't want to believe that Jesus was Your Son, Lord. They did not want the people to follow anyone but them because they wanted all the power. But power on earth is not so important when we think about Your heavenly kingdom, Lord. And the priests soon found that they couldn't stop people from loving Jesus— even by putting Him to death. Thank You for giving us Jesus, Lord, to love forever.

Prayer 351

Mark 14

Peter was scared that he would get caught too, so three different times he denied knowing Jesus. Jesus had predicted this would happen! Peter was one of Jesus' most loyal followers, but even he buckled under the pressure of Jesus' enemies. Dear Lord, I pray that I will always be proud to say, "I know Jesus!"

Prayer 352

Matthew 27

Dear God, Judas made a big mistake when he turned Jesus in for money. He realized too late that the money meant nothing to him because of the way he'd gotten it. But You would even have forgiven Judas if he had asked You. Please help us not to be tempted by money, dear Lord. Friendship and love are far more important than anything money can buy. Also, please help us to understand that we should never give up hope because You will forgive us even when we have done wrong.

Prayer 353

Luke 23

Pontius Pilate, the Roman governor, said Jesus wasn't a criminal. Pilate wanted to set Him free, but sadly, this wasn't to be. It makes me sad that Jesus had this chance to go free and wasn't allowed to. Please help me understand that You had a plan that even Jesus understood. I pray that leaders will learn to stick up for what they think is right, even if it's not the most popular way, Lord.

Prayer 354

Matthew 27; Luke 23

Pilate let the people decide what would happen to Jesus. He let them know that he was against their decision to crucify Jesus and let Barabbas go free. But Pilate still didn't go against their wishes. Please help me to have the courage to stand up for what I believe, Lord.

Prayer 355

Matthew 27

Dear Lord, making fun of others is cruel. The soldiers beat Jesus and made ugly jokes about Him. I pray that I'll think about Jesus and what He suffered the next time I want to play a dirty trick on someone. Please help me to look out for those who can't help themselves, Lord.

Prayer 356

Mark 15

Dear God, two criminals were crucified next to Jesus. One man said, "If You really are Jesus, why don't You save Yourself and us, too?" He was the type who would only believe in Jesus if he saw a big, showy miracle. But the other man told the first thief to have more respect for the Lord. He believed in Jesus, so Jesus told him he could join Him in heaven. Thank You, Lord, for showing Your mercy to everyone who believes in You.

Prayer 357

Mark 15; John 19

Before He died, Jesus forgave everyone who had hurt Him. Some people had hurt

His feelings by making fun of Him and even betraying Him. Others, like the Roman soldiers, had caused Him physical pain. It must have been very difficult for Jesus to forgive them because death on the cross is very painful. Dear God, please help me learn how to forgive. When someone hurts me on purpose or by accident, I pray that I can find the strength in my heart to forgive him.

Prayer 358

Luke 23; John 19

Dear God, after Jesus died, all of His followers were very sad. They had seen Jesus do so many miraculous things, but He still had to die. When things get really bad, we need our faith most of all, dear Father. Please bring us close to You when sad times come. Give us Your comfort and blessing.

Prayer 359

Matthew 28

When Mary and Mary Magdalene went to Jesus' tomb, what a wonderful sight it must have been to see that He wasn't there! Jesus had risen. Thank You, Lord, for bringing Jesus back to life! You made Your plan complete so everyone could have a chance to be saved. Praise You, Heavenly Father!

Prayer 360

Luke 24

Dear God, the disciples thought Mary and Mary Magdalene were seeing things when they said Jesus was alive. Some people still can't believe it's true. I pray that people everywhere will know that Jesus is the living Savior!

Prayer 361

Luke 24

When Jesus appeared to the disciples, He still did things the same way He had done before, Lord. He said the blessing before He ate and took time to talk about Bible Scriptures. Lord, I pray that I will take time in my day to do these things that were so important to Jesus.

Prayer 362

John 20

Dear God, even when the disciples told Thomas they had seen Jesus alive, he did not believe them. Thomas said he had to see Jesus for himself. There are still many "doubting Thomases." They don't believe anything unless it's right there in front of them. But many things exist that can't be seen—love, kindness, and joy, for example. True faith goes beyond what we can see. I believe in You, Lord. Even though I can't see You, I feel You in my heart. Thank You for Your love that lasts forever.

Prayer 363

John 21

Dear Lord, once, when the disciples were out fishing, a man appeared and asked them if they'd caught anything. When they said no, He asked them to cast their nets out again. The nets came back full of fish! Once again, Jesus had given those He loved all the food they could ask for. Then, He took Peter aside and asked him to "feed His flock." Jesus wanted Peter to look after the others because He would soon be going up to heaven. Dear God, I know Jesus wants us to take care of each other today the way Peter and the disciples took care of the people after Jesus rose to heaven. I pray that I never forget Jesus' wishes.

Prayer 364

Acts 1

Dear Lord, here is a poem about Your son.

Jesus rose up to heaven,
A long way from our sight.
He's with His Father now,
Sitting at His right.
Someday the clouds will open,
Like the day that follows night.
Jesus will come to earth again,
And the world will feel His might.

Prayer 365

Acts 1–2

Dear God, thank You for everything You've done for me. Thank You for sending Your Son so I can be forgiven for my sins. Please help me and guide me through Your Holy Spirit all the days of my life. I ask this in the name of Your Son, Jesus Christ. Amen.